BEYOND THINKING

Translators

Reb Anderson

Edward Brown

Norman Fischer

Blanche Hartman

Taigen Dan Leighton

Alan Senauke

Kazuaki Tanahashi

Katherine Thanas

Mel Weitsman

Dan Welch

Michael Wenger

Contributing Translator

Philip Whalen

Beyond Thinking
A Guide to Zen Meditation

Zen Master Dogen

Edited by Kazuaki Tanahashi
Introduction by Norman Fischer

SHAMBHALA
Boston & London
2004

SHAMBHALA PUBLICATIONS, INC.
Horticultural Hall
300 Massachusetts Avenue
Boston, Massachusetts 02115
www.shambhala.com

14 13 12 11 10 9 8 7 6

Printed in the United States of America

⊛ This edition is printed on acid-free paper that meets the American National
Standards Institute z39.48 Standard.

♻ Shambhala Publications makes every effort to print on recycled paper.
For more information please visit www.shambhala.com.

Distributed in the United States by Penguin Random House LLC
and in Canada by Random House of Canada Ltd

LIBRARY OF CONGRESS CATALOGING-IN-PUBLICATION DATA

Dogen, 1200–1253.
Beyond thinking: a guide to Zen meditation/Zen Master Dogen;
edited by Kazuaki Tanahashi.—1st ed.
p. cm.
Includes bibliographical references.
ISBN 978-1-59030-024-4 (pbk.: alk. paper)
1. Meditation—Sōtōshū. 2. Sōtōshū—Doctrines. I. Tanahashi,
Kazuaki, 1933– II. Title.
BQ9449.D652 2004
294.3'4435—dc22
2003024954

To Zenshin Ryufu Philip Whalen
1923–2003

whose life paralleled the history of Zen in America from his
involvement in the 1950s in Buddhism and Beat poetry, to his
studies in Japan in the 1960s, to his ordination as a Zen priest in
1972, to his subsequent teaching for thirty years.

His work with us in translating Dogen was just one of many
contributions to bringing Zen to America.

Contents

ZAZEN IN COMMUNITY

ZAZEN THROUGH THE SEASONS

Preface and Acknowledgments

EIHEI DOGEN (1200–1253) wrote practical instructions on meditation for beginners and adepts, which are still enormously useful in our time. Much of his extensive writing comes from and refers to advanced experiences of *zazen* or meditation in sitting posture. Although monk Dogen simply called his teaching the "buddha way," he has been regarded as founder of the Soto School, one of the two major schools of Zen Buddhism in Japan.

For this book we have selected his essays, talks, and instructions that touch on various aspects of Zen meditation. We present the text in four parts: "Entering Zazen," "Zazen Experience," "Zazen in Community," and "Zazen through the Seasons."

One of the foremost thinkers and writers in Japanese history, Dogen elucidates his teaching in an imaginative and paradoxical way. Some of his "linguistic somersaults" reflect his freedom from dualistic thinking and conventional logic. It could take one many years to make sense of some of his lines. Thus, *Beyond Thinking* is for advanced practitioners of meditation as well as for beginners.

It is stunning to see how much of his basic and practical instructions has been followed in Japan until now and how much of it is being adopted by Zen centers in the Western world. In the Introduction, Norman Fischer discusses the value of Dogen's teaching to those who practice Zen today, as well as some points that do not seem to be relevant any longer.

Beyond Thinking is the third Dogen book project of San Francisco Zen Center, following *Moon in a Dewdrop* and *Enlightenment Unfolds*. For details of Dogen's life, philosophy, and writings, please refer to the previous books.

We have tried to make our translations faithful to the original expressions and accessible to anyone who practices meditation or wants to do so. So, in some cases we have translated the Japanese words *kekka fuaza* as "sitting in cross-legged position," which is close to the original. But in other cases we have translated it as "sitting in meditation posture" because this is more inclusive of those who are unable to sit in traditional ways. We have translated *hishiryo* as "beyond thinking" and "nonthinking" because both English terms have advantages and limitations. The interchangeable use of the two terms can give a fuller transmission of meanings from one language to another. We have indicated examples of using two translated terms for one original term in our glossaries. I hope some of the glossary definitions will be helpful in "decoding" the apparently enigmatic expressions for which Dogen is renowned.

I feel extremely privileged to have had the opportunity to work with my cotranslators, who are all Zen teachers and fine writers. Each of the innumerable sessions of translating a text with one of my partners has been, without exception, a tremendously joyous learning experience. I am particularly grateful to Norman Fischer, who has written the excellent Introduction; to Taigen Daniel Leighton, who did scholarly editing and updating of the Selected Bibliography with his extensive knowledge; and to Dan Welch, who put an amazing amount of energy into editing the entire text, examining every word meticulously, and challenging the rest of the translators with alternative suggestions.

My gratitude goes to those who have participated in the Dogen seminars I facilitated in the past three years. Their valuable suggestions helped us to improve our draft translation. I would like to thank the roshis and senseis, who are the spiritual leaders of the Zen centers that hosted the seminars: Richard Baker (Dharma Sangha Europe and Crestone Mountain Zen Center); Chozen and Hogen Bays (Great Vow Zen Monastery); Kyogen and Gyokuko Carlson (Dharma Rain Zen Center); Joan Halifax (Upaya Zen Center); Blanche Hartman, Linda Ruth Cutts, and Paul Haller (San Francisco Zen Center, Green Gulch Farm, and Tassajara Zen Mountain Center); Enkyo O'Hara (Village Zendo); Katherine Thanas (Santa Cruz Zen Center and Monterey Bay Zen Center); and Jisho Warner (Stone Creek Zendo).

I would also like to thank Vicki Austin, president, and all the staff of San Francisco Zen Center for their continuous support of the Dogen translation project. Michael Wenger, Dean of Buddhist Studies and head of publication, conceived *Beyond Thinking* and has overseen the project. I appreciate Michael Katz as always for his counsel on turning a manuscript into a book. I would also like to thank Jeffrey Schneider, Eric Greene, Minette Mangahas, Julie Burtis, Nathan Wenger, and Linda Hess for their help. The drawings were done by Stephen Whitney.

Our Dogen study has benefited from centuries of Japanese scholarly commentaries and textual criticism. First and foremost, the *Shobogenzo* translation of Dr. Fumio Masutani into modern Japanese has been very useful. The works by colleagues of Dogen studies in the United States have also helped deepen our understanding; I particularly thank Dr. Carl Bielefeldt, Dr. Steven Heine, John Daido Loori Roshi, and Shohaku Okumura Roshi. As always, it has been wonderful to work with the staff of Shambhala Publications. My particular thanks to Peter Turner, Dave O'Neal, Steve Dyer, and Hazel Bercholz for their continuous help.

Notes to the Reader

Transliteration
Chinese terms are represented by the Pinyin System, which is the official way of transliteration in the People's Republic of China. Sanskrit words are simplified and their diacritical marks are omitted. Macrons for Sanskrit and Japanese words are used only in the glossaries.

Names
The abbots of Zen monasteries were often called by the name of the mountain, monastery, or region where they resided. Monasteries are sometimes represented by the names of the mountains on which they were located.

Dates
This book follows the lunar calendar, used traditionally in East Asia. The first to third months correspond to spring, and the other seasons follow in three-month periods. The fifteenth day of the month is the day of the full moon. (An extra month was occasionally added to make up a year.)

Years
Even though approximately the last thirty days of each lunar year run into the next solar year, to avoid confusion, we equate the entire lunar year to its corresponding solar year.

Time

See the diagram on page 110.

Age

A person is one year old at birth and gains a year on New Year's Day.

Notes

Translators' short notes are presented in brackets in the main text. An asterisk indicates the word(s) being explained in the Glossary of Terms or Names.

Texts and Translation Credits

All the texts in this book are translated from materials published in Doshu Okubo's *Dogen Zenji Zenshu (The Entire Work of Zen Master Dogen)*. We have also referred to *Dogen Zenji Zenshu*, edited by Tokugen Sakai, et al. The "Editor" refers to Kazuaki Tanahashi.

"Recommending Zazen to All People" (p. 3)
Known as *"Fukanzazengi"* in Japan, this is one of the most revered texts in the Soto School, as it summarizes Dogen's intention for establishing the Zen teaching in Japan. As the colophon states, he wrote this text in Chinese in 1227, the year of his return from China to Japan. His own calligraphed text, dated 1233, still exists. We present the version edited by Dogen later, which is included in *The Extensive Record of Eihei (Eihei Koroku)*.

Translated by Edward Brown and the Editor.

"Rules for Zazen" (p. 7)
Titled *"Zazengi,"* this short piece was written in Japanese and presented to his community in residence at the Yoshimine Temple in 1243, the year they moved from the Kosho Horin Monastery, south of Kyoto, to Echizen Province. This was when the Daibutsu Monastery was under construction. This text is one of the twenty fascicles of *The Treasury of the True Dharma Eye*

(*Shobogenzo*) that he wrote in the second half of the year in Echizen. ("Fascicle" is a chapter or a part of a book, originally bound in an independent bundle.)

Translated by Dan Welch and the Editor.

"Informal Talks" (p. 9)
Dogen calls an informal talk *yawa*, which literally means an "evening talk." These are excerpts from *The Treasury of the True Dharma Eye: Record of Things Heard (Shobogenzo Zuimonki)*, written in Japanese. Ejo collected the main materials for this book during the Katei Era (1235–1238) at the Kosho Horin Monastery, but some of his students completed the book after his death, based on his notes and words.

Translated by Michael Wenger and the Editor.

"On the Endeavor of the Way" (p. 12)
The original title of this text is *"Bendowa."* Dogen completed this writing on the day of the harvest moon in 1231. It was four years after his return from China, and two years before the founding of his first practice center, Kosho Horin Monastery. This text reflects his earliest attempt to express his thinking through writings in the Japanese language. It is also among the earliest attempts by Japanese Buddhist teachers to write in Japanese; until then, Buddhist teachings had been almost exclusively studied and written in the Japanese form of Chinese.

"On the Endeavor of the Way" is highly revered in the Soto School, as it is the most comprehensive elucidation of dharma throughout Dogen's teaching career. But Dogen did not put the words *The Treasury of the True Dharma Eye* at the beginning of its title. And when he edited *The Treasury of the True Dharma Eye* later, he did not include this fascicle in either the seventy-five-fascicle version or the twelve–fascicle version. The reason why Dogen put aside this text may be that the focus of his teaching moved toward training a small number of committed students as his community had matured, while this essay reflects his strong intention to spread dharma broadly.

According to Menzan Zuiho's *Eliminating Wrong Views on The Treasury of the True Dharma Eye* (*Shobogenzo Byakujakuketsu*, 1738), the text had been handed down in a courtier's house in Kyoto. Manzan Dohaku included this piece in the appendix of his eighty-four-fascicle version of *The Treasury of the True Dharma Eye* in 1684. Abbot Kozen of the Eihei Monastery included the fascicle in his ninety-five-fascicle version of *The Treasury of the True Dharma Eye*, published by the monastery in 1690, as its opening fascicle.

Translated by Lewis Richmond and the Editor.

"The Point of Zazen" (p. 37)

As its colophon states, this fascicle, "*Zazengi*," was written in Japanese at the Kosho Horin Monastery in 1242. Dogen brought it to Echizen and presented it at the Yoshimine Temple a year and half later. As with many other fascicles of *The Treasury of the True Dharma Eye*, this piece was presented to the assembly in the form of *jishu*, which is a dharma talk. It is likely that Dogen's jishu consisted mainly of reading his manuscript to the group of practicing students.

Translated by Michael Wenger and the Editor; Dogen's poem by Philip Whalen and the Editor.

"King of Samadhis" (p. 50)

This short piece was written in Japanese as part of *The Treasury of the True Dharma Eye*. It was presented to the assembly of the Yoshimine Temple on the fifteenth day, the second year of 1244. This was probably the most prolific moment in Dogen's life, as another fascicle called "Entire Body of the Tathagata" *(Nyorai Zenshin)* was presented on the same day, following the presentation of two other fascicles, "Arousing Unsurpassable Aspiration" *(Hotsu Mujoshin)* and "Arousing Aspiration for Enlightenment" *(Hotsu Bodaishin)* on the previous day.

Translated by Norman Fischer and the Editor.

"One Bright Pearl" (p. 54)
Its original title is *"Ikka Myoji."* Dogen presented this text to the assembly of the Kosho Horin Monastery in 1244. It was the third day of the practice period of that year, which was the third year since his first practicing center was established.

Written in Japanese, it is the fourth fascicle of *The Treasury of the True Dharma Eye*, following "On the Endeavor of the Way," "Maha Prajna Paramita" (Maka Hannya Haramitsu), and "Actualizing the Fundamental Point" (Genjo Koan). This is the only fascicle Dogen wrote in that year.

Translated by Edward Brown and the Editor.

"Dragon Song" (p. 59)
"Ryugin" is the last of the five fascicles of *The Treasury of the True Dharma Eye*, written in Japanese during the last two months of 1243. At this time, perhaps because of severe cold and heavy snowfall, Dogen's community was residing at a nameless building at the foot of Yamashi Peak, Echizen Province. They were already back to the Yoshimine Temple by the second month of the following year.

Translated by Mel Weitsman and the Editor.

"Great Enlightenment" (p. 63)
Also a fascicle of *The Treasury of the True Dharma Eye*, this was written in Japanese and presented to his community at the Kosho Horin Monastery in 1241 under the title *"Daigo."* It is one of the seventeen fascicles written there in that year. It was revised and presented for the second time at the Yoshimine Temple, Echizen, in the following year.

Translated by Blanche Hartman and the Editor.

"Ocean Mudra Samadhi" (p. 71)
A fascicle of *The Treasury of the True Dharma Eye*, this piece titled *"Kaiin Zammai,"* was written in Japanese at the Kosho Horin Monastery in 1242.

Translated by Katherine Thanas and the Editor.

"Awesome Presence of Active Buddhas" (p. 79)
"Gyobutsu Iigi," a fascicle of *The Treasury of the True Dharma Eye,* was written in Japanese in 1241. It was his tenth year of writing the monumental book, when eleven fascicles of it were completed.
Translated by Taigen Dan Leighton and the Editor.

"Regulations for the Auxiliary Cloud Hall" (p. 99)
Written in Japanese under the title *"Juundo Shiki"* at the Kosho Horin Monastery in 1239. The monastery's full name is *"Kannon-dori Kosho Horin Gokoku-ji"* (Guided by Avalokiteshvara's Merit, Raising Sages, Treasure Forest, Protecting the Nation Monastery). The long name of the monastery may reflect Dogen's wish to gain imperial patronage as a prayer temple for protection of the country. He soon seemed, however, to have abandoned the idea of seeking such patronage along with the name "Gokoku" (Protecting the Nation).

This piece was included in Kozen's ninety-five-fascicle version of *The Treasury of the True Dharma Eye* in 1690. But it had not been included in Dogen's seventy-five-fascicle or twelve-fascicle versions. Perhaps this text was intended to be used as practice guidelines for newcomers to the monastery who were not yet ready to reside and practice in the monks' hall.
Translated by Reb Anderson and the Editor.

"Guidelines for Practice of the Way" (p. 103)
The original title for this text is *"Bendo Ho."* The text is written in Chinese, as are the texts of most of his *shingi,* or monastic guidelines. Dogen wrote this text soon after his first full-scale practice place, the Daibutsu Monastery in Echizen, opened in 1244. It was included in *Monastic Guidelines of Eihei (Eihei Shingi)* after Dogen's death, and was first published in 1667.
Translated by Mel Weitsman and the Editor.

"Practice Period" (p. 118)
Titled *"Ango,"* this text was written in Japanese as a fascicle of *The Treasury of the True Dharma Eye.* It was presented to the

assembly of the Daibutsu Monastery in 1245, during its first summer practice period. After the completion of this fascicle, he only wrote three fascicles of *The Treasury of the True Dharma Eye* that he dated. His focus shifted toward compiling detailed monastic guidelines and giving formal talks to his practicing community.

Translated by Norman Fischer and the Editor.

"Formal Talks" (p. 143)

Fifteen *jodo* and one *shosan* are selected in this chapter. Jodo is an abbot's formal talk to the entire assembly of practitioners in the Zen tradition, which means "ascending the teaching seat in the hall." The hall may be the dharma hall in a full-scale monastery, otherwise it is in the monks' hall. Shosan, literally meaning minor meeting, is a less formal elucidation of dharma by the abbot to the assembly; it usually takes place in the abbot's quarter.

The source text is *The Extensive Record of Eihei (Eihei Koroku)*, compiled by Dogen's students. The first seven of the ten-fascicle text include 531 jodos presented by Dogen during the period between 1236 and 1252.

The dates and the places of the selected talks, as well as their sources—the fascicle numbers of the original text and their recorders—are as follows:

> The first day of the ninth month, 1246, Eihei (Monastery), f. 3, Ejo.
> The first day of the tenth month, 1242, Kosho Horin, f. 1, Senne.
> Winter solstice, 1240, Kosho Horin, f. 1, Senne.
> Enlightenment Ceremony, 1245, Daibutsu, f. 2, Ejo.
> Cutting the Arm Ceremony, 1250, Eihei, f. 5, Gien.
> New Year's Eve, year unknown, shosan, Eihei, f. 8, Ejo.
> New Year's Day, 1247, Eihei, f. 3, Ejo.
> The first full moon, 1247, Eihei, f. 3, Ejo.
> Nirvana Ceremony, 1247, Eihei, f. 3, Ejo.
> Closing the furnace, 1250, Eihei, f. 7, Gien.

Bathing the Buddha Ceremony, 1242, Kosho Horin, f.1,
Senne.

Starting the summer practice period, 1244, Daibutsu, f. 2,
Ejo.

Tango Ceremony, 1249, Eihei, f. 4, Ejo.

The first day of the sixth month, 1252, Eihei, f. 7, Gien.

End of the summer practice period, 1241, Kosho Horin,
f. 1, Senne.

The harvest moon, Eihei, 1250, f. 5, Gien.

Translated by Alan Senauke and the Editor.

Introduction

by Norman Fischer

THE YEAR 2000 MARKED THE 800TH ANNIVERSARY of Dogen's birth, a good time to appreciate the crucial contribution this great teacher has made not only to Japanese Soto Zen Buddhism, or even to Zen Buddhism in general, but also to religious practice the world over. The last half of the twentieth century has been perhaps the strongest time for Dogen's work: In Japan and in the West he has been studied as never before, and his thought has been influential not only for a Soto School that is now thoroughly international, but also in a wider philosophical discussion, in which he is often compared with Heidegger, Whitehead, Wittgenstein, and others.

Dogen's thought has proven useful and germane to many postmodern discussions in fields like metaphysics, epistemology, and language theory. When I began practicing Zen in 1970 and encountered Dogen's writing for the first time, he was very little known and understood in the West. Although much of his writing has yet to be brought into European languages, several English translations of his masterwork *Shobogenzo* (from which many of the pieces in this volume come), as well as other materials, are now available, and Western Zen practice centers based on his work have been established. With all this, I think we can say that serious study of Dogen in the West is well underway.

It seems natural then at this moment to take stock of where we stand with Dogen, both in Japan and in the West. Who is Dogen? What is his teaching? Why is he important? For those of us who have been practicing Zen for many years, studying and trying to put into practice Dogen's ideas, a new spirit is emerging. There is a greater willingness to view Dogen critically, to see the problems as well as the tremendous and sublime depths, and to recognize that the religion he founded has had its ups and downs. In Japan the Soto establishment has in recent years made a strong effort to reach out to the wider world. It has forthrightly apologized for past mistakes (supporting Japanese militarism before and during World War II and going along with the Japanese anti-Chinese racist policies of that period), and, more than this, it has engaged in its own internal debate about how and why these mistakes were made. In many ways the Japanese Soto church has made sincere efforts to accept non-Japanese practitioners not simply as colonial subjects of their religion, but also as robust and authentic practitioners in their own right, who may have something to contribute to a wider-ranging study of the master. All of this was unimaginable twenty-five years ago.

Western Zen practitioners are beginning to grow also, retaining a good deal of the initial wonder and adoration of Dogen, but tempering them with a critical eye. It is true that Dogen's writings are lofty, difficult, and profound, great treasures of world religious thought. And yet, we are now beginning to admit that Dogen's thought is also at times cranky, narrow-minded, elitist, fundamentalist, occasionally violent in its expression. We are beginning to admit that no human being, Dogen included, is perfect, unchanging, or always right, and that no person or institution remains unaffected by the social and political conditions that form the context for what happens to it.

Although Dogen was a religious reformer and innovator, he was also, deeply, a traditionalist. A traditionalist religious view is more often than not narrow-minded, authoritarian, and rule-bound, more likely to cut off real and vibrant life than to foster it. We need only study the record of any religious establishment to confirm this—from jihad to the Crusades, religion's effect on the human world has often been disastrous. And even when religion has fostered relatively peaceful times, it has often left scars of guilt and inner anguish on its most loyal adherents. Because of these tendencies, the last few hundred years have been understandably hard on traditionalist religion. The modern secular psychological and scientific viewpoint, which has taken religion as something old-fashioned and counterproductive to real human values, has been a source of liberation for many people.

But now that the developed world is, to a large extent, free of the old religion, and at the same time clearer about the limitations of the human species, the secular perspective is wearing thin. We are finding a new way to practice religion—not superficially, not rigidly, but flexibly and widely, lovingly not crabbily, with a gentle idealism that is not, as idealism all too often is, toxic.

One of the necessities of this new kind of religion is actual practice—daily practice. It is admirable and important to have the right ideas about our lives: to believe that goodness is possible and can be cultivated, to view compassion as the most important of human achievements, to want to be mindful not mindless, and so on. But these attitudes, wonderful as they are, aren't enough to carry us forward in the present world. We also need some concrete form of spiritual practice we can be committed to—an everyday practice that can be a strong basis for those beliefs and intentions and can help us to work with our daily conduct. By spiritual practice I mean activities that we actually do, that we take the time to do; activities that are, in a rational sense, useless, that are done merely for their own sake with no other goal or object; activities that are done with devotion and dedication to something larger than ourselves, and as much as possible without self-interest. Here is where Dogen's writings, particularly those included in this volume, which bear specifically on his understanding of meditation practice, can be immensely useful.

Soto Zen practice, Dogen's practice, centers on zazen, sitting meditation. But zazen is not, as one might imagine, a concentration technique to still the mind and produce religious insight. Dogen's zazen is much simpler and far more profound than that—even, as the reader will soon see, close to ineffable. I have always marveled at Dogen's sense of zazen practice. It is, on the one hand, extremely lofty and difficult, maybe even impossible to do, the most advanced and demanding of all possible spiritual practices; and, at the same time, it is a practice so easy and so accessible that anyone, no matter what his or her beliefs, skills, or level of commitment may be, can do—almost can't avoid doing. As Dogen says, zazen is a form of meditation so basic it can't even be called meditation. It is simply the practice of being what we are, of allowing, permitting, opening ourselves to ourselves. In doing that we enter directly the depth of our living—a depth that goes beyond our individual life and touches all life.

Dogen's zazen defies description or explanation. Though Soto Zen teachers sometimes offer practical suggestions about how to sit, they make it clear in their fuller discussions that zazen is no mere technique. Many have noted the paradoxical language (whose originator, as you will see, was Dogen himself) with which zazen is typically described. This is not to mystify the student— it's because there is no other way to speak of zazen accurately. The zazen that Dogen is advocating is neither devotional nor experiential; it's not a form of concentration or relaxation, though it may or may not include any or all these things. It is simply sitting in the midst of what utterly is, with full participation.

Dogen speaks to this in the very first sentence of the very first text he wrote explaining zazen, "Recommending Zazen to All People." If it is true that enlightenment is everywhere complete already, within us and outside us (as I suppose a theist would assert about God), then why would we need to do anything to bring it about? In fact, Dogen tells us, we do not. We practice zazen not to produce enlightenment but to express and manifest the enlightenment that is already there. As he says in "Rules for Zazen," zazen "is not conscious endeavor; it is not introspection." Still, there is a simple way to go about it. In this text Dogen goes on to explain exactly how to practice zazen—down to what temperature to maintain in the room, what to sit on, what to wear, and exactly how to arrange the body in the correct posture. The text is about a page long. It tells you all you need to know. Zazen practice is not difficult. Anyone can do it, and instruction takes only a few moments. Yet even many lifetimes are not long enough for it to mature.

Zazen is a physical practice. We don't usually think of spiritual practice as physical, and yet, life, soul, spirit, mind don't exist in the sky, they exist in association with a body. In Dogen's way of practice, body and mind (or spirit, soul) are one thing, and so to sit—to actually and literally sit down—paying close attention to the body as process, unifying consciousness and breathing with that process until you can enter it wholeheartedly—is to return naturally to what you most truly are. You have been this all along, whether you sit or not. But when you sit in zazen, you return to it and embrace it completely.

I suppose that the most widely quoted and misunderstood aspect of Dogen's zazen is the line that comes toward the end of this text: "[T]hink not thinking. How do you think not thinking? Nonthinking. This is the art of zazen." (Note that this term *hishiryo* can be rendered as "not thinking" or "nonthinking" or "beyond thinking." In this book the latter two renderings have been used, sometimes together. As is often the case in translating Dogen, whose use of terminology is often purposely multifaceted, one English word for one term is not sufficient to give the full flavor of the meaning.) I spent many years pondering this line— and practicing with it. It has turned out to be not so difficult to understand and to practice as I had thought. To think not thinking doesn't mean to stop thinking or to try to stop thinking. In saying "*think* not thinking," Dogen is talking about an alternative way to think—a way that is not enmeshed in desire and confusion but is rather fluid and free. Usually our thought is either dull and dim, or it is agitated. In both cases thought is being pushed by anxiety or desire. When we do zazen, we let go of all this, letting thinking simply rise and fall, by returning to awareness of breathing and posture. Thinking may be going on, but there's no more pushing—it's just thinking going on, not "I am thinking." This kind of thinking is what Dogen means by nonthinking, thinking beyond thinking. It is no problem. Sometimes in zazen there may not be any thinking, or very little of it. This is fine also.

In the final line of this short text, in a deceptively simple sentence, Dogen expresses the secret essence of his notion of zazen, and of all spiritual practice: "Zazen is the dharma gate of enjoyment and ease; it is undivided practice-enlightenment."

A great deal is said in these few words.

I think the real fruits of spiritual practice do not become apparent right away. If you do almost any kind of serious practice, even for a day or a weekend, you will see some powerful effects in your life. It is not at all unrealistic to think that someone can have a life-transforming experience in a short retreat or even in a morning at church. I have seen this happen many times. But the real fruits of spiritual practice grow over longer periods of time. As you go back day after day to your cushion, through times when you like it and times when you don't like it, times when it is very difficult to keep it up, times when your soul aches so badly you can't imagine sitting there for even a single moment more but you do it, and times when your mind is raging or your mind is so peaceful you can't believe there could ever be a troubled moment ever again—when you experience all of this year after year on your cushion, you begin to find a deep appreciation and satisfaction in your practice—and in your life. You feel as if your cushion is your home, your true spot, and that when you sit there, you are always all right. If you are a Buddhist, maybe you will say, "when I sit on my cushion I am sitting in the palm of Buddha's hand, and I feel this no matter what shape my mind is in"; and if you are a

Christian, you might say, "when I sit on my cushion I can feel Jesus' love flooding my heart." But whatever you say, I think that there will be a deep sense of satisfaction in your time of doing zazen, and not only then. You will feel that satisfaction in your life because you will know that you have come into contact with what is most basic and fundamental in the human heart: with love, letting go, and silence, and the taste of these will pervade your life. Even when the day comes when you lose everything to death, all your possessions, your friends, your body, your mind, even then, you will have some serenity knowing that the big mind, the larger reality, will always be present and will carry whatever you are to become exactly to where it needs to go.

By "undivided practice-enlightenment" Dogen means that our life is always whole. We have always been enlightened beings—this has always been the nature of our minds, the brightness of our consciousness. To really know this is to accept a deep responsibility, a joyful responsibility, for our living. For Dogen "practice-enlightenment" is one continuous event. It's not that we practice now in order to become enlightened later. Rather, because we have always been enlightenment, we must practice, and our practice is the expression of that enlightenment that is endless and beginningless.

Enlightenment is a lofty word, but its reality is something quite ordinary. The enlightened person is simply the person who isn't selfish, who sees things as they really are, loves them, and acts out of that love. With zazen practice we see a world that is lovely, and that calls out to us to participate in it. We are glad to do it. We can't not do it.

As you study the texts that make up this book and continue with your meditation practice, I think you will find difficulty in explaining or understanding what you are reading or experiencing. Dogen's expression of zazen practice, of human life, takes us to the very edge of what we can say or know. For Dogen there is no linear path connecting ordinary life to enlightened life, no scale of depth in living or understanding from superficial to profound. Each moment of practice is already the last as well as the first, and even a beginner is already finished. As he says in "On the Endeavor of the Way": "The zazen of even one person at one moment imperceptibly accords with all things and fully resonates through all time. . . . Each moment of zazen is equally wholeness of practice, equally wholeness of realization." In other words, in our daily zazen practice we entrust ourselves to the wholeness of our experience, to all of experience, moment by moment. We are not so much trying to calm down or improve as to give ourselves to the holiness that has always been at the center of our lives.

Although this is something we literally touch with our own bodies, as Dogen insists throughout his writing, it is not something we can know in the usual sense. We sense it, feel it, are it, as is true of everything else with which we come into contact throughout the course of our lives; and yet as soon as we think we know it as an object or an experience and begin to define or take credit for it, we lose track of it. In the same text Dogen says, "earth, grass, trees, walls, tiles, and pebbles . . . all engage in buddha activity," and inspired by them and in concert with them, we express the depths of what's true, unfolding widely inside the "endless, unremitting, unthinkable, unnameable buddha-dharma throughout the phenomenal world."

This is lofty indeed, and lest we get too excited about it and want to rush out with our good news to the world, Dogen reminds us that "it does not appear within perception, . . . because it is unconstructedness in stillness; it is immediate realization." Unconstructed. Immediate. This is how we begin to make efforts in our lives, then, inspired by our practice of zazen: letting go of our assumptions and preconceptions and coming forth in our lives from a stronger place. Not that we can ever eliminate our assumptions and preconceptions, but rather, that seeing them come and go in daily practice, we know them for what they are and can once and for all break their spell over our minds and hearts.

Passages such as these bring us face to face with one of the most often mentioned aspects of Dogen's writing: its difficulty.

We are speaking here not only of problems having to do with translation or cultural distance, but also with the sheer and inescapable fact that Dogen's writing, in places, is almost perversely opaque, to the point where one wonders whether he actually intends communication at all. For Dogen the central fact of our existence, and the source of its profundity as well as of the problems inherent in it, is that we are at once severely limited and, at the same time, limitless, and that these conditions depend on each other. In other words, as existent creatures we are bound by time and space, and yet also we have a foot in eternity, which is not a limitless span of time and space, but the true, imperceptible shape of each moment of our lives. Because this is Dogen's point over and over again, how can he not find himself immersed in linguistic spirals and verbal somersaults?

Underlying almost all Dogen has to say about meditation practice is this sensibility in regard to the paradoxical nature of time and space. As he says quite directly in "Ocean Mudra Samadhi": "Past moments and future moments do not arise in sequence. Past elements and future elements are not in alignment. This is the meaning of ocean mudra samadhi." (Samadhi is meditative concentration.) We experience ourselves conventionally, in the world of our own perception and emotion, as sequential, as within the realm of time and space. But the actual reality of time and space also must include nontime and nonspace, which is always present with us. To do zazen is to open ourselves to this reality.

For us, dying is the limit of time and space. Dying is present with us always, in the midst of every passing moment, although we usually do not think of it. Dogen thinks of it, and in doing so, how can he not come up against the limits of language, which is bound by time and space? So, in the text "King of Samadhis," for example, he cannot avoid expressions such as: "Know that the world of sitting practice is far different from other worlds. Clarify this for yourself, then activate the way-seeking mind, practice, enlightenment, and nirvana of the buddha ancestors. Study the world at the very moment of sitting. Is it vertical or horizontal? At the very moment of sitting, what is sitting? Is it an acrobat's graceful somersault or the rapid darting of a fish? Is it thinking or not thinking? Is it doing or not doing? Is it sitting within sitting? Is it sitting within body-mind? Is it sitting letting go of sitting within sitting, or letting go of sitting within body-mind? Investigate this in every possible way. Sit in the body's meditation posture. Sit in the mind's meditation posture. Sit in the meditation posture of letting go of body-mind."

These are not rhetorical questions; they are open questions, crucial questions. It is passages like this that have made me appreciate my practice and my life, hold myself always as open as I can to new possibilities of meaning and experience, and, incidentally, never tire of going back again and again to reading Dogen.

It is a very curious thing that this wonderful wide-open practice that Dogen so eloquently advocates became in his life and in the centuries afterward identified with a rigid and formalistic style of severe monasticism (the third part of this volume, "Zazen in Community," contains important texts that reflect this). Many readers of Dogen, baffled by this, choose to ignore or dismiss this as historical baggage, but to do so is to miss an important point.

The monastic life is strong. It involves dedication and total participation. There are no breaks, no hiding places, no profane moments. The monastic life honors a rule whose essence is simple: Always think of others and always act with others in mind, for we have no life without others. Dogen sees monastic life as the template life of the awakened person—he sees it as the life of the historical Buddha himself. In living the monastic life, we reenact ritually the Buddha's own life—our lives become his. The elaborately detailed rules and guidelines, the formalized bows and words, the minutely described marking out of sacred space through ceremony, the solemn rules, and gestures of seniority— all these serve to make this ritual life concrete through all our daily acts. Although most of us will not live in this way even for short periods of time, we can recognize the point that such way of life illuminates—that we are all Buddha in essence—and that every moment of our lives is a timeless crucial moment. And so we are challenged to live, making all our acts, large and small, buddha acts, because each and every one of our acts carries the moral, metaphysical, and symbolic weight of absolute truth.

For Dogen, monastic ritual is the way profound meditation practice can pervade our whole lives. This explains the elaborate rituals detailed so painstakingly in texts like "Guidelines for Practice of the Way" and "Practice Period," which can so easily sound hopelessly arcane to the modern reader. To translate them one virtually has to reconstruct maps of medieval Japanese monastic compounds, so detailed are they and so dependent on the physical layout of buildings and the texture of particular customs. How can such stuff be useful to us in our daily practice as twenty-first-century people?

One of the great casualties of modern life is the sense of coherent community. We all need to feel we belong to each other somehow, and when we do not feel that, our lives can feel broken, lonely, isolated, lacking in support, friendship, and love. The traditional structures for community (extended families living in close proximity to one another, an economic and social system that allows people to stay close to home on a daily basis, an agrarian- or crafts-based village life) are almost gone in much of the Westernized developed world and are probably not going to come back.

But I think it is possible for us to construct new forms of community that can replace or augment whatever remnants of this old community remain. Such new forms of community will require that we establish and maintain specific and sacred ways of doing things and of being together, ways that bind us closer and more profoundly than any casual or personal contact ever could. Although it is probably not possible or even desirable that we raise funds to construct detailed Japanese monastic establishments as Dogen describes them (as far as I know, none of the Western Zen monastic enclosures, even the major ones, have attempted this), we certainly can, through a lived understanding of the essentials of the monastic lifestyle, find ways to participate fully with each other in a sacred way. Once we train in such ways of conduct, we can apply the insights we have gained from them to our whole lives. In my own case, having spent a number of years living monastically, I can bring the deep structure and feel of that life to my daily life in the ordinary world. This training has helped me a great deal to learn how to include others in what I do and to feel that I am joined by others, even in my solitary acts.

For monastic life is fundamentally a life of participation with everything, and of kindness. Monastic renunciation is, in essence, letting go of the self-centered life. As Dogen says in "Regulations for the Auxiliary Cloud Hall," we should all be together "like milk and water," as grateful to each other for our mutually supportive practice as we are to our parents for our very life. It is this sense of communal sharing in gratitude that characterizes the monk's life, and that stands behind all that may strike us as archaic in Dogen's monastic writing. This inspired life of sharing and gratitude is also, in the final analysis, the essence of Dogen's understanding of meditation practice.

ENTERING ZAZEN

RECOMMENDING ZAZEN*
TO ALL PEOPLE

THE ESSENTIAL WAY FLOWS EVERYWHERE; how could it require practice* or enlightenment?* The essential teaching is fully available; how could effort be necessary? Furthermore, the entire mirror is free of dust; why take steps to polish it? Nothing is separate from this very place; why journey away?

And yet, if you miss the mark even by a strand of hair, you are as far apart from it as heaven from earth. If the slightest discrimination occurs, you will be lost in confusion. You may be proud of your understanding and have abundant realization, or you may have acquired outstanding wisdom and attained the way by clarifying the mind. However, even with high aspirations, if you wander about and get an initial glimpse of understanding, you may still lack the vital path that allows you to leap free of the body.

Observe the example of Shakyamuni Buddha* at the Jeta Grove,* who practiced upright sitting for six years even though he was gifted with intrinsic wisdom. Still celebrated is the Master Bodhidharma* of Shaolin Temple,* who sat facing the wall for nine years, although he had already received the mind seal.* An-

*Terms found in the Glossary carry an asterisk in their first occurrence.

cient sages were like this; who nowadays does not need to practice as they did?

Stop searching for phrases and chasing after words. Take the backward step and turn the light inward.* Your body-mind of itself will drop away* and your original face* will appear. If you want to attain just this,* immediately practice just this.

For zazen, a quiet room is appropriate. Drink and eat in moderation. Let go of all involvements and let myriad things rest. Do not think good or bad. Do not judge right or wrong. Stop conscious endeavor and analytic introspection. Do not try to become a buddha.* How could being a buddha be limited to sitting or not sitting?

In an appropriate place for sitting, set out a thick mat and put a round cushion on top of it. Sit either in the full- or half-lotus posture.* For the full-lotus posture,* first place the right foot on the left thigh, then the left foot on the right thigh. For the half-lotus posture, place the left foot on the right thigh. Loosen the robes and belts and arrange them in an orderly way. Then place the right hand palm up on the left foot, and the left hand on the right hand, with the ends of the thumbs lightly touching each other.

Sit straight up without leaning to the right or left and without

Zazen posture.

bending forward or backward. The ears should be in line with the shoulders and the nose in line with the navel. Rest the tongue against the roof of the mouth, with lips and teeth closed. Keep the eyes open and breathe gently through the nose.

Having adjusted your body in this manner, take a breath and exhale fully, then sway your body to left and right. Now sit steadfastly and think not thinking. How do you think not thinking? Beyond thinking.* This is the essential art of zazen.

The zazen I speak of is not learning meditation. It is simply the dharma gate* of enjoyment and ease. It is the practice-realization* of complete enlightenment. Realize the fundamental point* free from the binding of nets and baskets.* Once you experience it, you are like a dragon swimming in the water or a tiger reposing in the mountains. Know that the true dharma* emerges of itself, clearing away hindrances and distractions.

When you stand up from sitting, move your body slowly and rise calmly, without haste. We understand from the past that going beyond the ordinary and sacred, where sitting and standing are effortless and boundless, depends solely on the power of zazen.

Furthermore, to bring forth the fundamental turning point* by raising a finger, a pole, a needle, or a mallet, or to precipitate realization with a whisk, a fist, a stick, or a shout cannot be understood by discriminatory thinking. How can it be understood by the use of supernatural powers?* Zazen is an awesome presence beyond form and description. How is it not the path prior to conception?

Thus, do not be concerned with who is wise and who is foolish. Do not discriminate the sharp from the dull. To practice wholeheartedly is the true endeavor of the way. Practice-realization is not defiled, not special. It is a matter for every day.

Now, in this human world and in other realms, in India and China, buddha ancestors* invariably have maintained the buddha seal* and upheld the teaching of zazen practice immersed in steadfastness. Although circumstances may vary in a thousand ways, just practice zazen, giving yourself fully to the realization of the way. Why give up the sitting platform of your own house and wander uselessly in the dust of a remote land? Once a wrong step is taken, you depart from the way.

Having received a human life, do not waste the passing moments. Already upholding the buddha way, why indulge in the sparks from a flint? After all, form is like a dewdrop on the grass, life is like a flash of lightning—transient and illusory, gone in a moment.

Honored practitioners of the way, do not grope for the elephant or doubt the true dragon.* Endeavor on the immediate and straightforward way. Revere the mind that goes beyond study with effortless effort and surpasses all doing. Experience the enlightenment of the buddhas and correctly inherit the samadhi* of the ancestors. Practice thusness* continuously, and you will be thus. The treasury will open of itself for you to use as you wish.

Rules for Zazen

Practicing Zen* is zazen. For zazen a quiet place is suitable. Lay out a thick mat. Do not let in drafts or smoke, rain or dew. Protect and maintain the place where you settle your body that settles you. There are examples from the past of sitting on a diamond seat* and sitting on a flat stone covered with a thick layer of grass. Day or night the place of sitting should not be dark. It should be kept warm in winter and cool in summer.

Set aside all involvements and let the myriad things rest. Zazen is not thinking of good, not thinking of bad. It is not conscious endeavor. It is not introspection. Do not desire to become a buddha. Let sitting or lying down drop away. Be moderate in eating and drinking. Mindful of the passing of time, engage yourself in zazen as though saving your head from fire. On Mt. Huangmei* the Fifth Ancestor practiced zazen to the exclusion of all other activities.

When sitting zazen, wear the kashaya* and use a round cushion. The cushion should not be placed all the way under the legs but only under the buttocks. In this way the crossed legs rest on the mat and the backbone is supported with the round cushion. This is the method used by all buddha ancestors for zazen.

Sit either in the half-lotus position or in the full-lotus position. For the full lotus put the right foot on the left thigh and the left foot on the right thigh. The toes should lie along the thighs, not extending beyond. For the half-lotus position, simply put the left foot on the right thigh.

Loosen your robes and arrange them in an orderly way. Place the right hand on the left foot and the left hand on the right

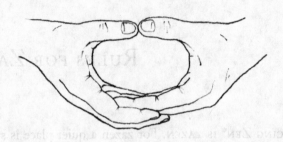

Zazen mudra.
This common hand position is called dharma world samadhi mudra.

hand, with the ends of the thumbs lightly touching each other. With the hands in this position, place them close to the body so that the joined thumb tips are at the navel. Straighten your body and sit erect. Do not lean to the left or right; do not bend forward or backward. Your ears should be in line with your shoulders, and your nose in line with your navel.

Rest your tongue against the roof of your mouth and breathe through your nose. Lips and teeth should be closed. Eyes should be open, neither too wide, nor too narrow. Having adjusted body and mind in this manner, take a breath and exhale fully.

Sit solidly in samadhi and think not thinking. How do you think not thinking? Nonthinking.* This is the art of zazen.

Zazen is not learning to do concentration. It is the dharma gate of great ease and joy. It is undivided practice-realization.

In the eleventh month, the first year of the Kangen Era [1243], this was taught to the assembly at the Yoshimine Temple,* Yoshida County, Echizen Province.

INFORMAL TALKS

*Recorded by Ejo**

ONE DAY DOGEN SAID:

While I was reading the recorded sayings of an ancient master in a monastery in China, a monk from Shu who was practicing the way said, "What's the use of reading such a book?"

I said, "I want to study the deeds of ancient masters."

He said, "What's the use of that?"

I said, "I hope to guide people when I go home."

He said, "What's the use of that?"

I said, "To benefit beings."

He said, " Ultimately, what's the use of that?"

Later, I thought about the meaning of his questions. I realized that reading recorded sayings and koans,* studying the deeds of ancient masters, and explaining them to the deluded are of no use for one's own development or in helping others. If you practice just sitting* and clarify the great matter—the essential meaning—your understanding becomes unlimited in guiding others, even if you don't know a single letter. That is why the monk said, "Ultimately, what's the use of that?"

Realizing he was right to the point, I stopped reading recorded sayings and other texts. I sat wholeheartedly and clarified the great matter.

One day I [Ejo] asked, "What is the spirit of practicing in a monastery?"

Dogen said, "Just sit. Practice continuous sitting in a hall or pagoda. Don't socialize, but sit like a deaf or a dumb person. Take joy in sitting harmoniously with yourself."

Dogen also said:
Do you attain the way with the mind or the body?

Those in the house of the scriptural schools say, "You attain the way with the body, because body and mind are one." But they are not clear about how the body directly attains the way. Now in our house [of Zen practice], body and mind together attain the way. As long as you try to figure out buddha-dharma* with mind, you can never attain it even for myriad eons or thousands of lifetimes. It is attained by letting go of the mind and abandoning views and interpretations. To see form and clarify the mind, to hear sound and come to realization is attainment of the way with the body.

Thus, when you practice just sitting and continuously give up all thoughts and views, the way becomes more and more intimate. So, attaining the way* means attaining it completely with the whole body. With this awareness you should sit wholeheartedly.

Dogen also said:
The primary point of awareness for those who practice the way is to be free from the idea of the self. To be free from the idea of the self means not to be attached to the self. Without being free from the self, the way of buddha ancestors cannot be attained, even if you master the words of ancient teachers and continue sitting like iron or stone for a thousand lifetimes in myriad eons. Further, mastering the expedient and complete teachings or exoteric and esoteric teachings without being free from attachment to the self would be like counting another's wealth without owning half a penny for oneself.

Practitioners of the way, I implore you, sit still and dispassionately contemplate the ephemeral nature of the body. The body, including hair and skin, is created from a drop from each of the parents. After the last breath is taken, the body is scattered over mountains and fields and turns into dirt. So, why attach to the body? If we examine the body in the light of dharma, what among the assembling and disassembling of the eighteen sense realms* can be determined as the self? Both within and outside scriptures, the ungraspable ephemeral nature of the body is used as a pointer for practice of the way. When you understand this, the true buddha way becomes evident.

ON THE ENDEAVOR OF THE WAY

ALL BUDDHA TATHAGATAS,* who individually transmit inconceivable dharma, actualizing supreme, perfect enlightenment, have a wondrous way, unsurpassed and unconditioned. Only buddhas transmit it to buddhas without veering off; receptive samadhi* is its mark. Sitting upright, practicing Zen, is the authentic gate to free yourself in the unconfined realm of this samadhi.

Although this inconceivable dharma is abundant in each person, it is not actualized without practice, and it is not experienced without realization. When you release it, it fills your hand—how could it be limited to one or many? When you speak it, it fills your mouth—it is not bounded by length or width.

All buddhas continuously abide in this dharma and do not leave traces of consciousness where they are. Sentient beings* continuously move about in this dharma, but where they are is not clear in their consciousness.

The concentrated endeavor of the way I am speaking of allows all things to come forth in realization to practice beyondness* in the path of letting go. Passing through the barrier [of dualism] and dropping off limitations in this way, how could you be hindered by nodes in bamboo or knots in wood [concepts and theories]?

After the thought of enlightenment arose, I began to search

for dharma, visiting teachers at various places in our country. Then, I met priest Myozen,* of the Kennin Monastery, with whom I trained for nine years, and thus I learned a little about the teaching of the Rinzai School.* Priest Myozen alone, as a senior disciple of ancestor Eisai,* correctly transmitted the unsurpassable buddha-dharma; no one can be compared with him.

Later, I went to Great Song China, visited masters on both sides of the Zhe River, and heard the teachings of the Five Houses.* Finally, I became a student of Zen master Rujing* of Taibo Peak* and completed my life's quest of the great matter.

Then, at the beginning of the Shaoding Era [1228–1233 CE] of Great Song, I came back to Japan with the vision of spreading the teaching and saving sentient beings—a heavy burden on my shoulders. And yet I have put aside the hope of having the teaching prevail everywhere until the time of rising opportunity. For the time being I wander about like a cloud or a water-weed, studying the wind of the ancient sages.

Yet, there may be true students who are not concerned with fame and gain, who allow their thought of enlightenment to guide them and earnestly desire to practice the buddha way. They may be misguided by incapable teachers and obstructed from the correct understanding, and intoxicated in confusion they may sink into the realm of delusion for a long time. How can they nourish the correct seed of prajna* and encounter the moment of attaining the way? Because I am wandering about, which mountain or river can they call on?

Because of my concern for them, I would like to record the standards of Zen monasteries that I personally saw and heard in Great Song, as well as the profound principle that has been transmitted by my master. I wish to leave for students of the way the authentic teaching of the buddha's house. This is indeed the essence:

The great master Shakyamuni entrusted dharma to Mahakashyapa* at the assembly on Vulture Peak*; it was then correctly transmitted from ancestor to ancestor down to the venerable Bo-dhidharma. Bodhidharma went to China and entrusted dharma to the great master Huike*; this was the beginning of dharma transmission* in the eastern country. In this way, by direct transmission, it reached Huineng,* the Sixth Ancestor, Zen Master Dajian. Then the authentic buddha-dharma spread in China, and the teaching that is not concerned with concepts and theories took form.

At that time there were two outstanding disciples of the Sixth Ancestor: Nanyue Huairang* and Qingyuan Xingsi.* They both equally received the buddha's seal, as guiding masters of human beings and devas.* Their two lineages spread, and later the Five Gates opened: the Fayan School,* the Guiyang School,* the Cao-dong School,* the Yunmen School,* and the Linji School.* At present in Great Song China, only the Linji School prospers throughout the country. But in spite of their different styles, each of the Five Houses holds the seal of the buddha mind.

In China after the Later Han Dynasty [25–220 CE], the teach-ings of Buddhist scriptures were introduced and spread all over the land, but there was no conclusive teaching as yet. When Bo-dhidharma came from India [527 CE], the root of twining vines was immediately cut off and the pure, single buddha-dharma spread. We should hope that it will be like this in our country.

Now, all ancestors and all buddhas who uphold buddha-dharma have made it the true path of unfolding enlightenment to sit upright practicing in the midst of receptive samadhi. Those who attained enlightenment in India and China followed in this way. Thus, teachers and disciples personally transmitted this ex-cellent method as the essence of the teaching.

In the authentic tradition of our heritage, it is said that this directly transmitted, straightforward buddha-dharma is the un-surpassable of the unsurpassable. From the first time you meet a master, without depending on incense offering, bowing, chanting buddha names, repentance, or reading scriptures, just wholeheart-edly sit, and thus drop away body and mind.

When even for a moment you sit upright in samadhi expressing the buddha's seal in the three activities [body, speech, and
thought], the whole phenomenal world becomes the buddha's
seal and the entire sky turns into enlightenment. Accordingly, all
buddha tathagatas increase dharma bliss, the original source, and
renew their magnificence in the awakening of the way. Furthermore, all beings in the phenomenal world of the ten directions*
and the six paths,* including the three lower paths,* at once obtain
pure body and mind, realize the state of great emancipation, and
manifest the original face. At this moment all things actualize
correct awakening; myriad objects partake of the buddha body;*
and sitting upright, a king under the bodhi tree,* they leap beyond
the boundary of awakening. Immediately, all things turn the un-
surpassably great dharma wheel* and expound the profound wisdom, ultimate and unconditioned.

This broad awakening comes back to you and a path opens
up to help you invisibly. Thus, in zazen you invariably drop away
body and mind, cut through fragmented concepts and thoughts
from the past, and realize essential buddha-dharma. You cultivate
buddha activity at innumerable practice places of buddha tathagatas everywhere, provide the opportunity for everyone to engage in
ongoing buddhahood, and vigorously uplift the dharma of going
beyond buddha.

Because earth, grass, trees, walls, tiles, and pebbles of the
phenomenal world in the ten directions all engage in buddha activity, those who receive the benefits of wind and water are incon-
ceivably helped by the buddha's transformation, splendid and
unthinkable, and intimately manifest enlightenment. Those who
receive these benefits of water and fire widely engage in cultivating the buddha's teaching based on original realization.* Because
of this, all those who live with you and speak with you also receive
immeasurable buddha virtue and extensively unfold the endless,
unremitting, unthinkable, unnameable buddha-dharma throughout the entire phenomenal world.

All this, however, does not appear within perception. Because it is unconstructedness in stillness, it is immediate realization. If practice and realization* were two things, as it appears to an ordinary person, each could be recognized separately. But what can be met with recognition is not realization itself, because realization is not reached with a discriminating mind. In stillness, mind and object merge in realization and go beyond enlightenment. Nevertheless, in the state of receptive samadhi, without disturbing its quality or moving a single particle, you engage the vast buddha activity, the extremely profound and subtle buddha transformation.

Grasses, trees, and lands that are embraced by this way of transformation together radiate a great light and endlessly expound the inconceivable, profound dharma. Grass, trees, and walls bring forth the teaching for all beings—common people as well as sages—and they in accord extend this dharma for the sake of grasses, trees, and walls. Thus, the realm of self-awakening and awakening others invariably holds the mark of realization with nothing lacking, and realization itself is manifested without ceasing for a moment.

This being so, the zazen of even one person at one moment imperceptibly accords with all things and fully resonates through all time. Thus in the past, future, and present of the limitless universe, this zazen carries on the buddha's transformation endlessly. Each moment of zazen is equally wholeness of practice, equally wholeness of realization.

This is so not only while sitting. A hammer strikes emptiness before and after its exquisite sound permeates everywhere. How can it be limited to this time and space? Myriad beings all manifest original practice, original face; it is impossible to measure. Even if all buddhas of the ten directions, as innumerable as the sands of the Ganges, exert their strength and with the buddha wisdom try to measure the merit of one person's zazen, they will not be able to fully comprehend it.

Question 1: We have now heard that the merit of zazen is lofty and great. But an ignorant person may be doubtful and say,

"There are many gates for buddha-dharma. Why do you recommend zazen exclusively?"

Answer: Because this is the front gate for buddha-dharma.

Question 2: Why do you regard zazen alone as the front gate?

Answer: The great master Shakyamuni correctly transmitted this splendid method of attaining the way and all buddha tathagatas of the past, future, and present attain the way by practicing zazen. For this reason it has been transmitted as the front gate. Furthermore, all ancestors in India and China attained the way by practicing zazen. Thus, I now teach this front gate to human beings and devas.

Question 3: We understand that you have studied the path of the buddha ancestors and correctly transmit the tathagatas' excellent method. This is beyond the reach of ordinary thought. However, reading sutras* or chanting buddha's name must be a cause of enlightenment. How can zazen, just sitting uselessly doing nothing, be depended upon for attaining enlightenment?

Answer: If you think that the samadhi of all buddhas, their unsurpassable great method, is just sitting uselessly doing nothing, you malign the Great Vehicle.* Such misunderstanding is like saying there is no water when you are in the middle of the ocean. Just now, all buddhas sit serenely at ease in receptive samadhi. Is this not the actualization of vast merit? What a pity that your eye* is not yet open, that your mind is still intoxicated!

The realm of all buddhas is inconceivable. It cannot be reached by intellect—much less can those who have no trust or lack wisdom know it. Only those who have the great capacity of genuine trust can enter this realm. Those who have no trust are unable to accept it, however much they hear it. Even at the assembly on Vulture Peak, there were those who were told by Shakyamuni Buddha, "You may leave if you wish."

When genuine trust arises, practice and study with a teacher. If it does not, wait for a while. It is regrettable if you have not received the beneficence of the buddha-dharma.

Also, what do you understand of the merit attained by reading sutras, chanting buddha's name, and so on? It is futile to think that just moving the tongue and making a sound is meritorious Buddhist activity. If you regard these as the buddha-dharma, it will be further and further away.

Actually, the meaning of studying sutras is that if you understand and follow the rules of practice for sudden or gradual realization taught by the buddha, you will unmistakably attain enlightenment. In studying sutras you should not expend thoughts in the vain hope that they will be helpful for attaining realization.

To attempt to reach the buddha way by chanting buddha's name thousands of times is like foolishly trying to go south while heading north or to fit a square peg into a round hole. To be consumed with words and letters while ignorant of the way of practice is like a physician forgetting how to prescribe medicine—what use can it be? People who chant all the time are just like frogs croaking day and night in spring fields; their effort will be of no use whatsoever. Even worse off are those deluded by fame and gain who cannot give up such practices, because their acquisitiveness is so deep. Such people existed in the past; are there not even more today? What a pity, indeed!

Just understand that when a master who has attained the way with a clear mind correctly transmits to a student who has merged with realization, then the inconceivable dharma of the Seven Original Buddhas,* in its essence, is actualized and maintained. This cannot be known by those who study words. Therefore, set aside your doubt, practice zazen under a correct teacher, and actualize buddhas' receptive samadhi.

Question 4: The Lotus School* and the Avatamsaka School,* which have been transmitted to Japan, both expound the ultimate of Mahayana teaching. Furthermore, the teaching of the Mantra School* was directly transmitted by Vairochana* Tathagata to Vajrasattva,* and its lineage from teacher to disciple since then has not been disturbed. This teaching expounds "Mind itself is buddha,"* and "Everyone's mind becomes buddha." They also advocate the correct enlightenment of the Five Buddhas* within one sitting, instead of practice through many eons. It is regarded as the supreme buddha-dharma. What extraordinary aspect of the practice you mention makes you recommend it, disregarding the practice of other schools?

Answer: You should know that in the buddha's house we do not discuss superiority or inferiority of the teaching, nor do we concern ourselves with the depth or shallowness of the dharma, but only with the genuineness of practice.

There are those who, attracted by grass, flowers, mountains, and waters, flow into the buddha way; and there are those who, grasping soil, rocks, sand, and pebbles, uphold the buddha's seal. Although the boundless words of the buddha permeate myriad things, the turning of the great dharma wheel is contained inside a single particle of dust. In this sense the phrase "Mind itself is buddha" is the moon reflected on water, and the teaching, "Sitting itself is becoming buddha" is a reflection in the mirror. Do not be concerned with the splendor of the words. By showing the buddha ancestors' excellent way of direct transmission, I am just recommending the practice of the immediate realization of enlightenment, hoping that you will become a true practitioner of the way.

For the transmission of buddha-dharma, the teacher should be a person who has merged with realization. Scholars concerned with words and letters cannot do it; this would be like the blind leading the blind.

Those within the gate of the buddha ancestors' correct transmission venerate an accomplished adept who has attained the way and merged with realization and entrust this master with the upholding of buddha-dharma. Accordingly, when spirit beings of the visible and invisible realms come to pay homage, or when arhats* who have attained the fruits of realization come to inquire about the dharma, this master will not fail to clarify the means to illumine their mind-ground.* This is not known in other teachings. Buddha's disciples should study the buddha-dharma alone.

You should know that fundamentally you do not lack unsurpassed enlightenment, and you are replete with it continuously. But you may not realize it, and be in the habit of arousing discriminatory views, and regard them as real. Without noticing, you miss the great way and your efforts will be fruitless. Such discriminatory views create flowers of emptiness.

You may imagine the twelvefold causation of rebirth,* or the twenty-five existences,* and have such views as the Three or Five Vehicles,* and whether the buddha exists or not. But do not take up these views and regard them as the correct way of practicing buddha-dharma.

Instead, sit zazen wholeheartedly, conform to the buddha seal, and let go of all things. Then, leaping beyond the boundary of delusion and enlightenment, free from the paths of ordinary and sacred, unconstrained by ordinary thinking, immediately wander at ease, enriched with great enlightenment. When you practice in this way, how can those who are concerned with the traps and snares of words and letters be compared with you?

Question 5: Among the three learnings,* there is the practice of samadhi, and among the six perfections, there is the perfection of dhyana.* Both of these have been studied by all bodhisattvas from the moment of arousing the thought of enlightenment, and both are practiced by the clever and dull. The zazen you speak of seems to be something like this. Why do you say that zazen alone contains the true teaching of the Tathagata?*

Answer: Your question arises because the treasury of the true dharma eye, the single great matter* of the Tathagata, the unsurpassable great dharma, has been named the Zen [Dhyana] School.* You should know that the name "Zen [Chan] School" appeared in China and spread eastward. It was not heard of in India. When the great master Bodhidharma sat facing the wall at the Shaolin Monastery on Mt. Song for nine years, neither monks nor laypeople knew the buddha's true teaching, so they called him the Brahman who concentrated on zazen. Subsequently, all buddha ancestors of every generation always devoted themselves to zazen. Heedless laypeople who saw them, without knowing the truth, informally called them the Zazen School. Later, the word za—sitting—was dropped, and nowadays it is called the Zen School.

The meaning of this teaching has been made clear through the discourses of our ancestors. Do not identify zazen with the dhyana or samadhi of the six perfections or the three learnings.

The authenticity of the transmission of this buddha-dharma is unhidden through all time. Long ago, at the assembly on Vulture Peak, the Tathagata entrusted venerable Mahakashyapa alone with the unsurpassable great teaching, the treasury of the true dharma eye, the wondrous heart of nirvana.* This event was witnessed by devas in the heavenly world; do not doubt it. The buddha-dharma is protected by these devas and its merit does not decrease.

You should know that the practice of zazen is the complete path of buddha-dharma and nothing can be compared with it.

Question 6: Why, among the four bodily presences* taught in the buddha's house, do you emphasize sitting alone, recommend Zen samadhi, and expound entry into realization?

Answer: It is impossible to know completely the methods by which all buddhas from the past practiced and entered realization, one after another. It is hard to know, but if you look into it, all buddhas are engaged in zazen as the source of realization. Don't look for anything else.

An ancestor said, extolling it, "Zazen is the dharma gate of enjoyment and ease." Thus, we know that sitting practice, among the four bodily presences, is the way of enjoyment and ease. Thus, it is not merely the practice of one or two buddhas, but all buddha ancestors have practiced in this way.

Question 7: Although it is clear that those who have not yet realized buddha-dharma should practice zazen and attain realization, for those who have already understood the buddha's correct teaching, what should they expect from zazen?

Answer: Although we should not talk about dreams with careless people, nor give a boat-pole to a woodcutter, nevertheless I will give instruction about this.

To suppose that practice and realization are not one is a view of those outside the way; in buddha-dharma they are inseparable. Because practice within realization* occurs at the moment of practice, the practice of beginner's mind is itself the entire original realization.

When giving instruction for zazen practice, we say that you should not have any expectation for realization outside of practice, because this is the immediate original realization. Because this is the realization of practice, there is no boundary in realization. Because this is the practice of realization, there is no beginning in practice.

In this way, Shakyamuni Tathagata and venerable Mahakashyapa were both fulfilled by practice within realization; great master Bodhidharma and Huineng—ancestor Dajian—were drawn in and turned by practice within realization. The ancient way of abiding in buddha-dharma has always been like this.

Practice just here is not apart from realization. Fortunately, each one of us has individually inherited this wondrous practice-realization; each beginner's endeavor of the way brings forth original realization in the realm of the unconstructed. To cultivate this realization, which is inseparable from practice, buddha ancestors always caution you not to be lax in practice. Release this wondrous practice and original realization fills your hands. Liberate original realization and wondrous practice is upheld throughout your body.

As I personally saw in Great Song, the Zen monasteries in various places all had meditation halls, where five to six hundred, or even up to two thousand monks, practiced zazen day and night. When I asked the abbots* of these monasteries, masters who had inherited the seal of buddha mind, about the essential meaning of buddha-dharma, I was told that practice and realization are not two different things.

Therefore, I recommend to students who are already studying with a teacher, as well as all those distinguished people who seek for the truth of buddha-dharma, to practice zazen and endeavor in the way under the guidance of an authentic teacher, and investigate the teaching of the buddha ancestors without distinguishing between beginning or advanced, and without being concerned with ordinary or sacred.

An ancient ancestor once said, "It is not that there is no practice and no realization, it is just that they cannot be divided." It has also been said, "One who sees the way practices the way." Understand that practice is endeavor in the midst of attaining the way.

Question 8: In the past various teachers went to Tang China and became transmitters of the dharma and spread the scriptural teaching widely throughout Japan. Why did they ignore a practice such as you have described and introduce only scriptural teaching?

Answer: The reason these ancient teachers did not introduce this dharma is that the time was not yet ripe.

Question 9: Did those masters in ancient times understand this dharma?

Answer: If they had understood it, it would have spread.

Question 10: One master said:

> Do not grieve over birth and death.* There is an immediate way to be free from birth and death, namely, to know the principle that the nature of mind is permanent. It means that because this body is already alive, it will eventually die, but the mind-nature will not perish. You should recognize that mind-nature exists within your body and is not affected by birth and death. This is the inherent nature. The body is a temporary form; it dies here and is born there and is not fixed. Mind is permanent; it does not change through past, future, or present.
>
> To understand this is to be free from birth and death. If you understand this principle, you become free from ordinary birth and death and enter the ocean of mind-nature when your body perishes. When you flow into the ocean of mind-nature, you attain wondrous virtue comparable to all buddha tathagatas. Even though you realize this now, because your body is formed as a result of deluded actions in past lives, you are not the same as all sages. If you do not recognize this principle, you will go around in birth and death forever. Therefore, you should hasten to understand that mind-nature is permanent. If you just spend your whole life leisurely sitting, what can you expect?

Does such a statement as this accord with the path of all buddhas and ancestors?

Answer: The view you have mentioned is not at all the buddha-dharma, but rather the view of Senika,* an outsider, who said:

> There is a soul* in one's body, and this soul, on encountering conditions, recognizes good and bad, right

and wrong. To discern aching and itching, or to know pain and pleasure, is also this soul's capacity. However, when the body is destroyed the soul comes out and is born in another world. So it appears to be dead here, but because there is birth in another place, it is permanent without dying.

To follow this view and regard it as the buddha's teaching is more foolish than grasping a piece of stone and regarding it as gold. Such shameful ignorance cannot be compared to anything. National Teacher Huizhong* of Great Tang criticized this deeply. To take up the mistaken view that mind is permanent and forms perish, while regarding this as equal to the wondrous teaching of all buddhas, or to create the causes of birth and death while wishing to be apart from birth and death—is this not foolish? It is most pitiable. Just understand it as the mistaken view of someone outside the way and do not listen to it.

As I cannot refrain from being sympathetic, let me disabuse you of your mistaken view. In buddha-dharma it is always taught that body and mind are not separate, and that nature and characteristics are not two. This has been known throughout India and China, so there is no room for mistake. In fact, from the perspective of permanence, all things are permanent; body and mind are not separate. From the perspective of cessation, all things cease; nature and characteristics cannot be divided. How can you say body perishes but mind is permanent? Is it not against the authentic principle? Furthermore, you should understand that birth-and-death is itself nirvana. Nirvana is not realized outside of birth-and-death. Even if you think that mind is permanent apart from the body and mistakenly assume that the buddha's wisdom is separate from birth-and-death, the mind of this assumption still arises and perishes momentarily and is not permanent. Is it not truly ephemeral?

You should know that the teaching of the oneness of body and mind is always being expounded in the buddha-dharma.

How then can mind alone leave the body and not cease when the body ceases? If body and mind are inseparable sometimes and not inseparable at other times, the buddha's teaching would be false. To think that birth-and-death must be rejected is the mistake of ignoring buddha-dharma. You must refrain from this.

The so-called dharma gate of the whole reality of mind-nature in buddha-dharma includes the entire phenomenal world, without separating nature from characteristics or birth from death. Nothing, not even bodhi* or nirvana, is outside of mind-nature. All things and all phenomena are just one mind; nothing is excluded or unrelated. It is taught that all dharma gates are equally one mind, and there is no differentiation. This is the Buddhist understanding of mind-nature. How can you differentiate this into body and mind and separate birth-and-death and nirvana? Already you are buddha's child. Do not listen to the tongues of madmen, quoting an outsider's view.

Question 11: Should those who are entirely engaged in zazen strictly follow the precepts?

Answer: Holding to the precepts and pure actions is the rule of the Zen Gate and the teaching of buddha ancestors. Even those who have not yet received the precepts or have broken the precepts can still receive the benefit of zazen.

Question 12: Is it all right for those who practice zazen also to engage in chanting mantras* or in the practice of shamatha [calming the mind] and vipashyana [analytical introspection]?

Answer: When I was in China and inquired of masters about the essence of the teaching, I was told that none of the ancestors who correctly transmitted the buddha's seal in India and China in the past or present had ever engaged in such a combination of practices. Indeed, without devoting yourself to one thing, you cannot penetrate the one wisdom.

Question 13: Should zazen be practiced by laymen and laywomen, or should it be practiced by home-leavers* alone?

Answer: The ancestors say, "In understanding buddha-dharma, men and women, noble and common people, are not distinguished."

Question 14: Home-leavers are free from various involvements and do not have hindrances in zazen in pursuit of the way. How can members of the laity, who are variously occupied, practice single-mindedly and accord with unconstructed buddha-dharma?

Answer: Buddha ancestors, out of their kindness, have opened the wide gate of compassion in order to let all sentient beings enter realization. Who among humans and heavenly beings cannot enter?

If you look back to ancient times, the examples are many. To begin with, Emperors Dai* and Shun* had many obligations on the throne; nevertheless, they practiced zazen in pursuit of the way and penetrated the great way of buddha ancestors. Ministers Li* and Fang* both closely served their emperors, but they practiced zazen, pursued the way, and entered realization in the great way of buddha ancestors.

This just depends on whether you have the willingness or not. It does not matter whether you are a layperson or home-leaver. Those who can discern excellence invariably come to this practice. Those who regard worldly affairs as a hindrance to buddha-dharma think only that there is no buddha-dharma in the secular world; they do not understand that there is no secular world in buddha-dharma.

Recently, there was a high official of Great Song, Minister Feng,* who was an adept in the ancestors' way. He once wrote a poem concerning his view of practice:

> I enjoy zazen between my official duties,
> and seldom sleep lying on a bed.

Although I appear to be a minister,
I'm known as a Buddhist elder throughout the country.

Although he was busy in his official duties, he attained the way because he had a deep intention toward the buddha way. When considering someone like him, reflect on yourself and illuminate the present with the past.

In Song China, kings and ministers, officials and common people, men and women grounded their intention on the ancestors' way. Both warriors and literary people aroused the intention to practice Zen and study the way. Among those who pursued this intention, many of them illuminated their mind-ground. From this, we understand that worldly duties do not hinder the buddha-dharma.

When the true buddha-dharma is spread widely in the nation, the rule of the monarch is peaceful because all buddhas and devas protect it unceasingly. If the rule is peaceful, the buddha-dharma gains eminence.

When Shakyamuni Buddha was alive, even those who previously had committed serious crimes or had mistaken views attained the way. In the assemblies of the ancestors, hunters and woodcutters attained enlightenment. As it was so for them at that time, it is so for anyone now. Just seek the teaching of an authentic master.

Question 15: Can we attain realization if we practice, even in this last age of decline?

Answer: In the scriptural schools they explain various categories, but in the true Mahayana* teachings, dharma is not divided into periods of truth, imitation, and decline. Instead, it is taught that everyone attains the way by practice. Particularly, in this correctly transmitted teaching of zazen, you are fulfilled with the treasure you already have, entering dharma and leaving bondage behind. Those who practice know whether realization is attained or not, just as those who drink water know whether it is hot or cold.

Question 16: Someone once said:

> In buddha-dharma, if you comprehend the meaning of "Mind itself is buddha," that will be sufficient without any chanting of sutras or practicing the buddha way. To know that "buddha-dharma originally lies in the self" is the completion of attaining the way. Other than this, you need not seek from anyone else.

Why should you be troubled with practicing zazen and pursuing the way?

Answer: This statement is entirely groundless. If what you say were true, then whoever has a mind would immediately understand the meaning of buddha-dharma. You should know that buddha-dharma is realized by giving up the view of self and other.

If the understanding of "Self itself is buddha" were the attaining of the way, Shakyamuni Buddha would not have taken the trouble to elucidate the way. Let me illuminate this with an excellent case of an ancient master:

> Once a monk called Director Xuanze* was in the assembly of Zen master Fayan.* Fayan asked him, "Director Xuanze, how long have you been in my community?"
>
> Xuanze said, "I have been studying with you for three years."
>
> The master said, "You are a recent member of the community. Why don't you ask me about buddha-dharma?"
>
> Xuanze said, "I cannot deceive you, sir. When I was studying with Zen Master Qingfeng,* I mastered the state of ease and joy in buddha-dharma."
>
> The master said, "With what words did you enter this understanding?"
>
> Xuanze said, "When I asked Qingfeng, 'What is the self of a Zen student?' he said, 'The fire god is here to look for fire.'"
>
> Fayan said, "That is a good statement. But I'm afraid you did not understand it."

Xuanze said, "The fire god belongs to fire. So, I understood that fire looks for fire and self looks for self."

The master said, "Indeed, you did not understand. If buddha-dharma were like that, it would not have been transmitted until now."

Then Xuanze was distressed and left the monastery. But on his way he said to himself, "The master is a renowned teacher in this country, a great leader of five hundred monks. His criticism of my fault ought to have some point."

He went back to Fayan, apologized, and said, "What is the self of a Zen student?"

Fayan said, "The fire god is here to look for fire."

Upon hearing this statement, Xuanze had a great realization of buddha-dharma.

In this way we know that mere recognition of "Self itself is buddha" is not penetrating buddha-dharma. If the understanding of "Self itself is buddha" were buddha-dharma, Fayan would not have given such criticism or guidance. Just inquire about the rules of practice as soon as you meet the master, single-mindedly practice zazen, and pursue the way, without leaving a half-understanding in your mind. Then the excellent art of buddha-dharma will not be in vain.

Question 17: We have heard that in India and China there have been people in the past and present who realized the way on hearing the sound of bamboo being struck, or who understood the mind when seeing the color of blossoms. Great master Shakyamuni was awakened to the way when he saw the morning star, and venerable Ananda understood the dharma when a bannerpole fell down. Furthermore, after the Sixth Ancestor in China among the Five Houses, there were many who realized the mindground with one word or half a phrase. Not all of them necessarily practiced zazen in pursuit of the way; is this not so?

Answer: Of those who clarified the mind upon seeing a form, or who realized the way upon hearing a sound, not one had any discriminative thinking regarding the endeavor of the way or attached to self other than their original self.

Question 18: People in India and China by nature are refined. As they are in the center of civilization, when buddha-dharma is taught to them, they can immediately enter it. In our country since ancient times, people have been bereft of compassionate wisdom, and it is difficult for the right seed of prajna to be nourished. This is because we are uncivilized. Is it not regrettable? Thus, home-leavers in our country are inferior to even the laity in those great countries. Our entire nation is foolish and narrow-minded, and we are deeply attached to visible merit and are fond of worldly values. If such people do zazen, can they immediately realize buddha-dharma?

Answer: What you say is correct. Among people in our own country, compassionate wisdom does not yet prevail, and their nature is rather coarse. Even if the correct dharma is explained to them, its nectar becomes poisonous. Many easily pursue fame and gain, and it is difficult for them to be free from delusion.

However, entering into realization of buddha-dharma does not require the worldly wisdom of humans and devas as a boat for fleeing the world. When the Buddha was alive, someone realized the four fruits of attainment* when he was hit by a ball; another understood the great way by wearing a robe in jest. They were both ignorant people, like beasts, but with the aid of genuine trust they were able to be free from delusion. A laywoman serving food to an ignorant old monk, who was sitting in silence, was enlightened. This did not depend upon wisdom, scripture, words, or speech; it was only brought about by genuine trust.

Now, Shakyamuni Buddha's teaching has been spread in the billion worlds* for about two thousand years.[1] Those countries are

---

1. Recent scholarship indicates that Shakyamuni lived in the fifth century BCE, about 1,600 to 1,700 years before Dogen's time.

not necessarily the countries of compassionate wisdom, and the people are not necessarily sharp and intelligent. However, the Tathagata's true dharma in essence has a great inconceivable meritorious power and spreads throughout those countries when the time is ripe.

If you practice with genuine trust, you will attain the way, regardless of being sharp or dull. Do not think that buddhadharma cannot be understood in this country because this is not a country of compassionate wisdom and people are foolish. In fact all people have the seed of prajna in abundance; it is only that they have rarely realized it and have not yet fully received buddhadharma.

This exchange of questions and answers may have been rather confusing; a number of times flowers of emptiness were made to bloom. However, because the meaning of zazen in pursuit of the way has not been transmitted in this country, those who wish to know about it may be regretful. Therefore, for the sake of those who wish to practice, I have recorded some of the essential teachings of the clear-eyed teachers, which I acquired in China. Beyond this, guidelines for practice places and regulations for monasteries are more than I can mention now. They should not be presented casually.

Our country lies to the east of the dragon ocean, far from China, but the Buddha's teaching was transmitted eastward to Japan, about the time of Emperors Kimmei* and Yomei.* This is the good fortune of our people, yet the philosophy and rituals have been entangled, and authentic practice was not established. Now, if you make patched robes and mended bowls your whole life, build a grass-roofed hut near a mossy cliff or white rock, and practice sitting upright, you immediately go beyond buddha and directly master the great matter of your life's study. This is the admonition of Dragon Fang* [Longya], the transmitted way of practice of Mt. Rooster-foot [where Mahakashyapa practiced]. Concerning the method of zazen, I would refer you to "Recommending Zazen to All People," which I wrote during the Karoku Era [1225–1227 CE].

Although a king's edict is needed for spreading dharma in the country, if we think of the Buddha entrusting the dharma to kings and ministers on Vulture Peak, all the kings and ministers who have appeared in the billion worlds are born because of their wish from a previous birth to protect and guard buddha-dharma. Where this teaching prevails, is there any place that is not a buddha land? Thus, spreading the way of buddha ancestors does not depend upon place or circumstance. Just consider today as the beginning.

I have written this to leave for people of excellence who aspire for buddha-dharma and for true students who, wandering like water-weeds, seek the way.

Mid-autumn day [the fifteenth day of the eighth month] in the third year of the Kanki Era [1231], by Dogen, who has transmitted dharma from Song China.

Zazen Experience

THE POINT OF ZAZEN

YAOSHAN,* GREAT MASTER HONGDAO, was sitting. A monk asked him, "In steadfast sitting, what do you think?"

Yaoshan said, "Think not thinking."

The monk asked, "How do you think not thinking?"

Yaoshan replied, "Beyond thinking."

Realizing these words of Yaoshan, you should investigate and receive the correct transmission of steadfast sitting. This is the thorough study of steadfast sitting transmitted in the buddha way.

Yaoshan is not the only one who spoke of thinking in steadfast sitting. His words, however, were extraordinary. "*Think not thinking*" is the skin, flesh, bones, and marrow of thinking, and the skin, flesh, bones, and marrow of not thinking.

The monk said, "How do you think not thinking?" However ancient *not thinking* is, still we are asked how to think it. Is there not thinking in steadfast sitting? How can going beyond steadfast sitting not be understood? One who is not shallow or foolish can think and ask about steadfast sitting.

Yaoshan said, "Beyond thinking." The need for nonthinking* is crystal clear. In order to think not thinking, nonthinking is always used. In nonthinking, there is somebody that sustains you. Even if it is you who are sitting steadfast, you are not only thinking but are upholding steadfast sitting. When sitting steadfast, how can steadfast sitting think steadfast sitting? Thus, sitting steadfast is not buddha thought, dharma thought, enlightenment thought, or realization thought.

This teaching was transmitted from Shakyamuni Buddha to Yaoshan through thirty-six generations of ancestors. That means if you go back thirty-six generations from Yaoshan, there is Shakyamuni Buddha. What was correctly transmitted thus was "think not thinking."

However, careless students in recent times say, "The endeavor of zazen is completed when your heart is quiescent, as zazen is a place of calmness." Such a view does not even reach that of students of the Small Vehicles,* and is inferior to that of teachings of Human and Deva Vehicles.* How can we call them students of buddha-dharma? In present-day Song China, there are many practitioners who hold such views. The decline of the ancestral path is truly lamentable.

There are also people who say, "Practicing zazen is essential for those who are beginners or those who have started studying recently, but it is not necessarily the activity of buddha ancestors. Activity in daily life is Zen, and sitting is Zen. In speaking and in silence, in motion and stillness, your body should be tranquil. Do not be concerned only with the practice of zazen." Many of those who call themselves descendants of Linji hold such a view. They say so because they have not received the transmission of the right livelihood of buddha-dharma.

Who are beginners? Are there any who are not beginners? When do you leave beginner's mind? Know that in the definitive study of the buddha-dharma, you engage in zazen and endeavor in the way. At the heart of the teaching is a practicing buddha who does not seek to become a buddha. As a practicing buddha does not become a buddha, the fundamental point is realized. The embodiment of buddha is not becoming a buddha. When you break through the snares and cages [of words and concepts], a sitting buddha does not hinder becoming a buddha. Thus right now, you have the ability to enter the realm of buddha and enter the realms of demons throughout the ages. Going forward and going backward, you personally have the freedom of overflowing ditches, overflowing valleys.

Mazu,* Zen Master Daji Jiangxi, studied with Nanyue, Zen Master Dahui. After intimately receiving Nanyue's mind seal, Mazu was continuously engaged in zazen. One day Nanyue went up to him and said, "Virtuous one, what's your intention in doing zazen?"

Quietly ponder this question. Was Nanyue asking if Mazu had the intention of going beyond zazen, if he had an intention outside of zazen, or if he had no intention at all? Was Nanyue asking what kind of intention emerges while doing zazen? Investigate this thoroughly.

You should cherish a true dragon instead of a carved one. However, you should know that both carved and true dragons have the ability to produce clouds and rain. Do not treasure or belittle what is far away, but be intimate with it. Do not treasure or belittle what is near, but be intimate with it. Do not make light of or a big deal of what you see with your eyes. Do not make light of or a big deal of what you hear with your ears. Rather, illuminate your eyes and ears.

Mazu said, "My intention is to become a buddha."

You should clarify these words. What is the meaning of *become a buddha*? Does *become a buddha* mean being made buddha by another buddha, buddha making oneself buddha? Is this the emergence of one or two buddhas? Is the intention to become buddha dropping off, or is dropping off the intention to become buddha? Does this mean that however many ways there are to become buddha, to be immersed in this intention to become a buddha is the intention to become buddha?

Know that Mazu meant that zazen is invariably the intention to become buddha, and that zazen is invariably becoming buddha with intention. Intention is prior to becoming a buddha and after becoming a buddha. Intention is the very moment of becoming buddha.

I ask you: How much of becoming buddha is being immersed in intention? Immersion is always a direct expression of totally becoming buddha. This immersing brings forth more immersing, every bit of completely becoming buddha. It is bits and pieces of intention. Do not avoid intention. If you avoid it, you lose your body and miss your life. When you lose your body and miss your life, this too is immersion in intention.

Nanyue picked up a tile and started to polish it on a rock.

Mazu asked, *What are you doing?*

Indeed, who does not see this as polishing a tile? Who can see this as polishing a tile? So Mazu asked, *What are you doing? What are you doing?* is polishing a tile. Whether in this world or in another world, polishing a tile has never ceased. Thus, you should not regard your view as the only view. In any activity, there is always this question. Those who see buddha without knowing and understanding buddha see water without understanding water, and see mountains without knowing mountains. To hastily conclude that what's happening in front of you is a dead end is not a study of buddha.

Nanyue said, "I am polishing this tile to make a mirror."

Clarify these words. Polishing a tile to make a mirror has a deep meaning; it is not a false statement, but is actualizing of the fundamental point. Although a tile is a tile, and a mirror is a mirror, there are many ways to investigate the meaning of polishing. Even an ancient bright mirror comes from polishing a tile. Without knowing that all mirrors come from polishing tiles, you will not understand the words, mouth, or breath of buddha ancestors.

Mazu said, "How do you make a mirror by polishing a tile?"

Indeed, an iron-willed practitioner, by polishing a tile and doing nothing else, does not make a mirror. Even if making a mirror is not polishing a tile, a mirror is immediately there.

Nanyue said, "How can you become a buddha by doing zazen?" Be clear that zazen is not working toward becoming a buddha. The teaching that becoming a buddha has nothing to do with zazen is evident.

Mazu said, "Then, how so?"

These words may seem to be asking one thing but in fact are asking another. It is like close friends meeting; each is intimate with the other. *How so?* addresses both zazen and becoming a buddha at the same time.

Nanyue said, "When driving a cart, if it stops moving, do you whip the cart or the ox?"

In regard to driving a cart, what is moving and what is stopping? Does it mean that water flowing is the cart moving and water not flowing is the cart moving? You can also say that flowing is water not moving. There is a time when water's moving is not flowing. Thus, when you investigate the cart not moving, there is stopping and not stopping; it depends on time. The word "*stopping*" does not merely mean not moving.

In regards to Nanyue's words "*Do you whip the cart or the ox,*" is it that you sometimes hit the cart and sometimes hit the ox? Is hitting the cart the same or not the same as hitting the ox? In the secular world, there is no custom of hitting the cart. Although there is no custom of common people hitting the cart, in the buddha way there is the practice of hitting the cart; this is the eye of study. Even if you realize the practice of hitting the cart, it is not the same as hitting the ox. Study this thoroughly.

Although hitting the ox is commonly practiced, you should investigate hitting the ox in the buddha way. Is it hitting a living buffalo, an iron ox, or a clay ox? Is it hitting with a whip, with the entire world, or with the whole mind? Is it hitting the marrow, hitting with the fist? How about fist hitting fist, and ox hitting ox?

Mazu was silent.

Do not ignore this silence. This is hurling a tile to attract a jewel, turning the head and turning the face. This silence cannot be taken away.

Nanyue then instructed: "When you practice sitting Zen, you practice sitting buddha."

Investigate this statement and understand the pivotal point

of the ancestral school. Those who miss the essential meaning of the practice of sitting Zen may say that it is the practice of sitting buddha. But how can those who are not authentic descendants be sure that the practice of sitting zazen is the practice of sitting buddha? Know that the zazen of beginner's mind is the beginning of zazen. The beginning of zazen is the beginning of sitting buddha.

Nanyue continued: "When you practice sitting Zen, you will know that Zen is not about sitting or lying down."

What Nanyue meant is that zazen is zazen, and it is not limited to sitting or lying down. This teaching has been transmitted person to person; thus boundless sitting and lying down are the self [beyond self]. When you reflect on your life activities, are they intimate with zazen, or remote from it? Is there enlightenment or is there delusion in zazen? Is there one whose wisdom penetrates zazen?

Nanyue said further, "In the practice of sitting buddha, the buddha has no fixed form."

Nanyue explained sitting buddha in this way. The reason why sitting buddha is neither singular nor plural is that the sitting buddha is adorned with no fixed form. To speak of no fixed form is to speak of buddha's form. As buddha has no fixed form, there is no escape from sitting buddha. Adorned with buddha's no fixed form, the practice of zazen is itself sitting buddha. In the dharma of no abiding, who can discriminate buddha from not buddha? Falling away before discrimination, sitting buddha is sitting buddha.

Nanyue said, "When you sit buddha, you kill [go beyond] buddha."

When we study sitting buddha further in this way, it has an aspect of *killing buddha*. At the very moment of sitting buddha, there is *killing buddha*. If you want to find the extraordinary luminosity of killing buddha, always sit buddha. *Killing* may be an ordinary word that people commonly use, but its meaning here is totally different. Study the deep meaning behind the statement that sitting buddha is *killing buddha*. Investigate the fact that the function of buddha is itself *killing buddha*, and study "killing" and "not killing" a true person.

Nanyue said, "If you are identified with the sitting form, you have not reached the heart of the matter."

To be *identified with the sitting form*, spoken of here, is to let go of and to touch the sitting form. The reason is that when one is sitting buddha, it is impossible not to be one with the sitting form. However clear the sitting form is, the heart of the matter cannot be reached, because it is impossible not to be one with the sitting form. To penetrate this is called letting go of body and mind.

Those who have not practiced sitting do not reach the heart of the matter. The heart of the matter is sitting time, sitting person, sitting buddha, and the practice of buddha. In most cases, sitting of sitting and lying down is not sitting buddha. Although usual sitting looks like sitting buddha or buddha sitting, it is not so. A person becomes buddha, becoming a buddha person. However, all people do not become buddhas. Buddhas are not all people, because buddhas are not limited to people. An ordinary person is not necessarily buddha, buddha is not necessarily an ordinary person. Sitting buddha is like this.

In this way, Nanyue was a profound teacher and Mazu was a thorough student. Mazu realized sitting buddha as becoming buddha, and Nanyue taught becoming buddha as sitting buddha. At Nanyue's assembly there was this kind of investigation, and at Yaoshan's assembly there was that dialogue. Know that what buddhas and ancestors have regarded as the pivotal point is sitting buddha. Those who are buddha ancestors employ this pivotal point. Those who aren't have never dreamed of it.

Transmission of buddha-dharma in the west and east [India and China] is no other than transmission of sitting buddha. This is the pivotal point. Where buddha-dharma is not transmitted, zazen is not transmitted. What has been passed on person to person is the essential teaching of zazen alone. Those who have not intimately received this teaching are not buddha ancestors.

Without clarifying this single dharma, you cannot clarify myriad dharmas and practices. Without clarifying dharmas and practices, you cannot be regarded as one who has attained the way with clear eyes and cannot join the buddha ancestors of past and present. Thus, buddha ancestors invariably receive and transmit zazen person to person.

To be illuminated by buddha ancestors is to endeavor in the thorough practice of zazen. Those who are ignorant mistakenly think that buddha light is like sunlight, moonlight, or the glowing of a jewel. But sunlight, moonlight, or the glowing of a jewel is merely a physical manifestation in the transmigration through the six paths*, and cannot be compared with buddha light. Buddha light is to receive and listen to one phrase of teaching, to maintain and guard one dharma, and to transmit zazen person to person. Without being illuminated by such light, accepting and maintaining zazen is not possible.

Since ancient times, few have understood zazen as it is. Even the heads of famous monasteries in China nowadays do not know and investigate the meaning of zazen. There are only a few who clearly understand it. Monasteries have schedules for zazen, the abbots and resident monks keep the practice of zazen as essential, and encourage students to practice zazen. But few of them seem to understand the meaning of what they are doing.

Some masters have written texts titled "Essentials of Zazen," a few others have written "Rules for Zazen," and a few more have written "The Point of Zazen." Among these none of the texts titled "Essentials of Zazen" are worthwhile. No version of "Rules for Zazen" clarifies the practice. They were written by those who did not know zazen as they had not received the transmission of zazen person to person. "The Point of Zazen" included in *Jingde Record of Transmission of the Lamp** and "Essentials of Zazen" included in *Jiatai Record of the Universal Lamp** are also like this. What a pity! They visited monasteries in the ten directions and practiced all their lives, but they did not make a thorough effort even for one sitting. Sitting had not immersed in them and endeavor had not encountered them. It is not that zazen avoided them, but that they were carelessly intoxicated. They did not aspire to a genuine thorough effort.

Their texts merely aim to return to the source and origin, trying to cease thinking and to be still. That does not even come up to taking the steps of visualization, purification, nurturing, and attainment, or the view of the bodhisattvas' last ten stages* approaching buddha's enlightenment. How could they have received and transmitted the buddha ancestors' zazen? The Song Dynasty compilers of Zen texts included these writings by mistake. Those who study now should not pay attention to such writings.

"The Point of Zazen," written by Zhengjue, Zen Master Hongzhi* of the Tiantong Jingde Monastery, Mt. Taibo, Qingyuan Prefecture, China, alone is a work of a buddha ancestor. It is a true point of zazen, with penetrating words. It is the only light that illuminates the inside and outside of the phenomenal world; it is buddha ancestor among buddha ancestors of past and present. Earlier buddhas and later buddhas have been led to zazen by this teaching. Present buddhas and past buddhas are actualized by this "The Point of Zazen." The text is as follows:

The hub of buddhas' activity,
the turning of the ancestors' hub,
is known free of forms
illuminated beyond conditions.

As it is known free of forms
knowledge is subtle.
As it is illuminated beyond conditions
illumination is wondrous.

When knowledge is subtle
there is no thought of discrimination.

When illumination is wondrous
there is not the slightest hint.

Where there is no thought of discrimination
knowledge is extraordinary with no comparison.
Where there is not the slightest hint
illumination has nothing to grasp.

Water is clear to the bottom
where the fish swims without moving.
The sky is vast and boundless
where the bird flies away and disappears.

The point presented here is the manifestation of great function, the awesome presence beyond sound and form, bamboo knots and wood grains [standards] before the parents were born. It is joyously not slandering buddha ancestors, not avoiding the death of body and mind. It is as extraordinary as having a head that is three feet tall and a neck that is two inches short.

The hub of buddhas' activity: Buddhas do not fail to make buddhas the hub. This hub is manifested. That is zazen.

The turning of the ancestors' hub: One's master's words are incomparable. This understanding is the basis of ancestors, of transmitting dharma, and of transmitting the robe. Turning heads and exchanging faces is the hub of buddhas' activity. Turning faces and exchanging heads is the turning of the ancestors' hub.

Is known free of forms: This knowing is not, of course, conscious knowing. Conscious knowing is small. This knowing is not comprehension. Comprehension is created. Thus, this knowing is free of forms. Being free of forms is this knowing. Don't regard it as all-inclusive knowledge. Don't limit it to self-knowledge. Being free of forms is "When brightness [duality] comes, meet it with brightness. When darkness [nonduality] comes, meet it with darkness," "Sit through the skin you were born with."

Illuminated beyond conditions: This illumination is not illuminating everything or illuminating with brilliance. Being beyond conditions is this illumination. Illumination does not change into conditions, as conditions are already illumination. *Beyond* means the entire world is not hidden, a broken world does not appear. It is subtle and wondrous. It is interchangeable and beyond interchangeable.

When knowledge is subtle there is no thought of discrimination: Thought as knowledge does not depend on other power. Knowledge is a shape, and a shape is mountains and rivers. The mountains and rivers are subtle. The subtle is wondrous. When you utilize it, it is lively. When you create a dragon, it is not limited inside or outside of the dragon gate. To utilize a bit of this knowledge is to know by bringing forth mountains and rivers of the entire world, using all your force. If you don't have knowledge by being intimate with mountains and rivers, there is not a shred or scrap of knowledge. Do not grieve that discernment and discrimination come slowly. Buddhas who have already discerned are already being actualized. *There is no thought of discrimination* means there is already merging. There is already merging is actualization. Thus, *there is no thought of discrimination* is not meeting even one person.

When illumination is wondrous there is not the slightest hint: *The slightest* is the entire world. The illumination is naturally wondrous and luminous. Thus, it looks as if it hadn't arrived. Do not doubt your eyes. Do not believe your ears. To directly clarify the source beyond words and not to grasp theories through words is illumination. This being so, illumination is not comparing, not grasping. To maintain illumination is extraordinary and to accept it as complete is no other than investigating it thoroughly.

Water is clear to the bottom where the fish swims without moving: Water hanging in the sky does not get to the bottom. Furthermore, water that fills a vessel is not as clear as the water mentioned here. Water that is boundless is described as *clear to the bottom*. When the fish swims in this water, it goes for myriad miles. There is no way to measure it, and there is no shore to limit it. There is no sky for the fish to fly in and no bottom to get to, and there is no shore where someone sees the fish. In fact, there is no one who sees the fish. If you speak of recognizing the fish, there is merely water clear to the bottom. The function of zazen is just like the fish swimming. Who can measure how many thousands and myriad of miles there is in zazen? Its journey is the entire body traveling the path where no bird flies.

The sky is vast and boundless where the bird flies away and disappears: The vast sky does not hang above. What hangs above is not called the vast sky. Furthermore, what encompasses all space is not called the vast sky. What is neither revealed nor hidden, neither inside nor outside is called the vast sky. If the bird flies in this sky, it just flies in the sky. The practice of flying in the sky is immeasurable. Flying in the sky is the entire world; the entire world is flying in the sky. Although we don't know how far the flying goes, we say it beyond saying—we say "away." It is "Go away with no string on your straw sandals." When the sky flies away, the bird flies away. When the bird flies away, the sky flies away. When you speak about investigation of flying, it is right here. This is the point of steadfast sitting. Even if you go myriad miles, it is right here.

This is "The Point of Zazen" by Zhengjue. Among the old masters throughout time, no one has written "The Point of Zazen" like this. If the stinky skin bags* here and there would try to say something like this, they might not be able to do so in one or more lifetimes. Now, there is no text other than Zhengjue's. Rujing, my late master, would refer to him on his teaching seat as Old Buddha Hongzhi and would not refer to other teachers as Old Buddha. One who has the eye to see a true person recognizes the voice of buddha ancestors. Thus we know that there is a buddha ancestor in the lineage of Dongshan.*

More than eighty years have passed since the time of Zhengjue. After his text, I have written my version of "The Point of Zazen." It is the eighteenth day, the third month, the third year of the Ninji Era [1242]. It has been eighty-five years since Zhengjue passed away on the eighth day, the tenth month, the twenty-seventh year of the Shaoxing Era [1157].

This is my text:

THE POINT OF ZAZEN

The hub of buddhas' activity,
the turning of the ancestors' hub,
moves along with your nonthinking
and is completed in the realm of nonmerging.*

As it moves along with your nonthinking
its emergence is immediate.
As it is completed in the realm of nonmerging
completeness itself is realization.

When its emergence is intimate
there is no separateness.
When completeness reveals itself
it is neither real nor apparent.

When there is immediacy without separateness
immediacy is "dropping away" with no obstacle.
Realization, beyond real or apparent,
is effort without desire.

Clear water all the way to the ground;
a fish swims like a fish.
Vast sky transparent throughout;
a bird flies like a bird.

Although Zhengjue's text is not incomplete, zazen may be spoken of in this way. All descendants of buddha ancestors should practice zazen as the single great matter. It is the authentic seal transmitted from person to person.

Written at the Kosho Horin Monastery* on the eighteenth day, the third month, the third year of the Ninji Era [1242]. Presented to the assembly at the Yoshimine Temple, Yoshida County, Echizen Province, in the eleventh month of the fourth year of the Ninji Era [1243].

King of Samadhis

To transcend the world directly, to manifest the magnificence of the buddha ancestors' house—this is sitting in the meditation posture. To leap over the heads of outsiders and demons, and become a true person inside the buddha ancestors' room—this is sitting in the meditation posture. To sit in the meditation posture is to transcend the deepest and most intimate teaching of the buddha ancestors. Thus, buddha ancestors practice this way without needing to do anything else.

Know that the world of sitting practice is far different from other worlds. Clarify this for yourself, then activate the way-seeking mind,* practice, enlightenment, and nirvana of the buddha ancestors. Study the world at the very moment of sitting. Is it vertical or horizontal? At the very moment of sitting, what is sitting? Is it an acrobat's graceful somersault or the rapid darting of a fish? Is it thinking or not thinking? Is it doing or not doing? Is it sitting within sitting? Is it sitting within body-mind? Is it sitting letting go of sitting within sitting, or letting go of sitting within body-mind? Investigate this in every possible way. Sit in the body's meditation posture. Sit in the mind's meditation posture. Sit in the meditation posture of letting go of body-mind.

Rujing, my late master, Old Buddha, said, "Practicing Zen is letting go of body and mind. It can only be done by wholehearted sitting; incense offering, bowing, chanting Buddha's name, repentance, and sutra reading are not pivotal."

My late master is the only one in four or five hundred years who has plucked out the eye of the buddha ancestors, and sat down inside that eye. There are few in China who can stand shoulder to shoulder with him. Perhaps, there are some who have understood that sitting is buddha-dharma and buddha-dharma is sitting. And perhaps, there are some who have personally experienced that sitting is buddha-dharma. But there is no one else who has personally experienced that sitting is sitting, and so there is no one else who upholds buddha-dharma as buddha-dharma.

Thus, there is sitting with the mind, which is not the same as sitting with the body. There is sitting with the body, which is not the same as sitting with the mind. There is sitting letting go of body-mind, which is not the same as sitting letting go of body-mind. To get to this place is to be immersed in the practice and understanding of the buddha ancestors. Maintain this insight. Investigate this awareness.

Shakyamuni Buddha said to the assembly, "When you sit in the meditation posture, you realize samadhi in body and mind, and give rise to an awesome virtue that people respect. Like the sun illuminating and refreshing the world, this sitting removes obscurities from the mind and lightens the body so that exhaustion is set aside. Enlightenment becomes as natural as a dragon curled up at rest. A demon is frightened even by a picture of someone sitting in the meditation posture; how much more so by a living person who realizes the way sitting motionless and at ease."

As the Buddha said, a demon is startled and frightened by even a picture of someone sitting in the meditation posture and even more frightened by a living person sitting that way. So, we know that the merit of such sitting is immeasurable. This ordinary everyday sitting is itself boundless joy.

Shakyamuni Buddha continued speaking to the assembly, "Therefore, you should sit in the meditation posture."

Then the Tathagata, the World-honored One,* taught his disciples how to sit and said to them, "Some outsiders try to practice by standing on tiptoes, others by standing continuously, and still others by adopting the yogic posture of hooking their feet over their shoulders. These people develop unbalanced minds that founder in an ocean of delusion because their postures are unnatural. Why do I teach my disciples to sit up straight in the meditation posture? Because it is easy to regulate the mind when the body is upright. If the body is straight, the mind is not dull. Instead, the mind is forthright, the intention is true, and mindfulness is present. If the mind scatters or the body leans, gather together your body-mind and resume the upright posture. If you want to manifest samadhi and enter it, you should gather together all distracted thought and scattered mind within this posture. Practice in this way and you will manifest and intimately enter the king of samadhis."

Thus, we clearly know that sitting in the meditation posture is itself the king of samadhis. It is itself manifesting and intimately entering. All other samadhis serve the king of samadhis.

Sitting in the meditation posture is a forthright body, a forthright mind, a forthright body-mind, a forthright buddha ancestor, a forthright practice-realization, a forthright top of the head, and a forthright life stream. When you sit in the meditation posture, the skin, flesh, bones, and marrow of a human being are immediately vivid in the king of samadhis. The World-honored One always sat in this meditation posture and correctly transmitted it to all his disciples. The World-honored One taught humans and devas how to sit in this meditation posture. It is the mind seal correctly transmitted by the Seven Original Buddhas.

Shakyamuni Buddha sat in this meditation posture under the bodhi tree for fifty small eons, sixty great eons, and innumerable unclassifiable eons. Perhaps, he sat for three weeks, or maybe only for a few hours. In any case, the Buddha's zazen is the turning of the wondrous wheel of dharma; in it is contained his lifetime guidance. Nothing is lacking. The yellow scrolls and red rolls of the sutras are all here. In this moment of sitting, buddha sees buddha and all beings attain buddhahood.

Soon after Bodhidharma, the First Chinese Ancestor, arrived from India, he sat zazen, facing the wall in the meditation posture for nine years at the Shaolin Temple, Shaoshi Peak of Mt. Song. Since then, the head and eyeball* of his practice have prevailed all over China. Bodhidharma's life stream is just this sitting in the meditation posture. Before he came from India, people in China had not truly known sitting in the meditation posture. But after he arrived, they came to know it. Thus, for one lifetime, for myriad lifetimes, from head to toe, without leaving the monastery and without concern for other activities, wholeheartedly sit in the meditation posture day and night—this is the king of samadhis.

Presented to the assembly of the Yoshimine Temple on the fifteenth day, the second month, the second year of the Kangen Era [1244].

ONE BRIGHT PEARL*

XUANSHA,* GREAT MASTER ZONGYI, of Mt. Xuansha, Fu Region, China of the Saha World,* used to be called Shibei. His family name was Xie.* When he was a householder, he loved fishing and boating on the Nantai River, doing as fishermen do. One day at the beginning of the Xiantong Era [860–873], a golden-scaled fish came to him without his seeking for it, and he suddenly had the urge to leave the dusty world. So, he gave up his boat and went off into the mountains. He was thirty years old when he realized the precariousness of the floating world and the preciousness of the buddha way. Then, he went to Mt. Xuefeng and studied with Xuefeng,* Great Master Zhenjue, endeavoring in the way day and night.

One day, as he was leaving the mountain with his traveling bag to visit other monasteries to further his study, his toe hit a rock and began to bleed. In sharp pain he suddenly had a realization and said to himself, "If my body doesn't exist, where does this pain come from?" So, he went back to see Xuefeng.

Xuefeng said, "What's with the traveling bag, Bei [Shibei]?"

Xuansha said, "No one can be fooled."

Xuefeng appreciated his words and said, "Who doesn't know these words, yet who else could say them?" Then he said, "Why doesn't Bei with the traveling bag go and study all over?"

Xuansha said, "Bodhidharma didn't come to China. Huike didn't go to India."

Xuefeng praised him.

Although Xuansha was a fisherman who had never read sutras, he focused on his intention to practice and was strongly determined. Xuefeng saw his practice excel in the community and regarded him as an outstanding student. The coarse cotton robe Xuansha wore all the time was worn and tattered, so he wore a paper robe under it. He sometimes added dried mugwort grasses to cover himself. He did not study with anyone other than Xuefeng. Thus, he acquired the capacity to inherit Xuefeng's dharma.

Some years after attaining the way, Xuansha instructed his students, saying, "The entire world of the ten directions is just one bright pearl."

Once a monk asked him, "I heard that you said, 'The entire world of the ten directions is just one bright pearl.' How can I understand this?"

Xuansha said, "The entire world of the ten directions is just one bright pearl. What do you do with your understanding?"

The next day Xuansha asked the monk, "The entire world of the ten directions is just one bright pearl. How do you understand this?"

The monk said, "The entire world of the ten directions is just one bright pearl. What do you do with your understanding?"

Xuansha said, "I know that you have worked out a way to get through the demon's cave on the black mountain."

Xuansha first spoke the words *the entire world in the ten directions is just one bright pearl*. The meaning is that the entire world in the ten directions is neither vast nor minute, neither square nor round. It is not neutral, not active, and not obvious. Because it is not birth and death coming or going, it is birth and death coming and going. Thus, past days have already left here and the present moment starts from here. When we investigate the entire world in the ten directions, who can see it as bits and pieces, who can talk about it as ceaseless activity?

The entire world in the ten directions means that you ceaselessly chase things and make them into the self, and you chase the self and make it into things. When emotions arise, wisdom is pushed aside. By seeing this separation, teacher and student turn their heads and exchange their faces, unroll the great matter and harmonize their understanding. Because you chase the self and make it into things, the entire world of the ten directions is ceaseless. Because you move ahead, you do more than distantly see the essential matter.

One bright pearl is not yet a name but an expression of understanding. Although there have been people who thought it was only a name, one bright pearl directly experiences ten thousand years. While the entire past has not yet departed, the entire present is just now arriving. Here is the now of the body and here is the now of the mind. This is the bright pearl; it is not limited to grass and trees here and there, or even to mountains and rivers in the universe.

How can I understand this? These words appear to be the monk's expression of ignorance, but the great function emerges right here, actualizing the great principle. Step forward and penetrate one foot of water, one foot of wave—ten feet of pearl, ten feet of illumination.

In expressing his understanding, Xuansha said, *The entire world in the ten directions is just one bright pearl. What do you do with your understanding?* These words are an expression that buddhas inherit from buddhas, ancestors inherit from ancestors, and Xuansha inherits from Xuansha. If you do not want to inherit this expression, there may be a way not to do so. But even if you totally avoid it for a while, this expression arises all-inclusively right now.

The next day Xuansha asked the monk, *The entire world of the ten directions is just one bright pearl. How do you understand this?* This is an expression that takes up yesterday's statement and adding another layer, blows it back today. His question today pushes down yesterday's nodding. The monk said, *The entire world of the ten directions is just one bright pearl. What do you do with your understanding? Speak!* This is the horse of a robber on horseback chasing the robber. An authentic buddha speaking to you walks in the midst of various beings. Now, turn the light inward and illuminate yourself. How many ways do you understand this? You may say "seven layers of milk cake" or "five layers of herb cake." Yet, there is teaching and practice south of Xiang, north of Tan* [both in Hunan Province].

Xuansha said, *Now I know that you have worked out a way to get through the demon's cave on the black mountain.* Know that the sun face and moon face have not changed since ancient times. The sun face emerges with the sun face, and the moon face emerges with the moon face. So, even in the sixth month [height of summer], do not say your nature is hot. The timeless thusness of this one bright pearl is boundless. It is just that the entire world of the ten directions is one bright pearl, not two or three. The entire body is one true dharma eye, the true body, a single phrase. The entire body is illumination; the entire body is the entire mind. When the entire body is the entire body, there is no hindrance. A gentle curving turns round and round.

With the power of the bright pearl manifesting in this way, Avalokiteshvara* and Maitreya* see form and hear sound; old buddhas and new buddhas reveal their bodies and expound dharma. At this very moment the bright pearl hangs in space or is sewn inside the robe*; it is hidden under the chin or in the hair. This is one bright pearl, the entire world in the ten directions. Although it is sewn inside the robe, do not try to hang it outside the robe. Although it is hidden under the chin or in the hair, do not try to take it out.

A man sewed a valuable pearl inside the clothes of a dear friend who was drunk [as told in the *Lotus Sutra*]. A dear friend always gives a valuable pearl. When a pearl is sewn inside one's clothes, one is always drunk. This is one bright pearl, the entire world in the ten directions. All things, turning or not turning while drunk, are one bright pearl. Knowing the bright pearl is one bright pearl. This is how it is with one bright pearl.

This being so, although you may say, "I am not a bright pearl," you should not doubt in this way. Whether you doubt it or not, such doubt comes from a limited view. Limited views are merely limited views.

How lovely are one bright pearl's infinite colors and shades! Bits and pieces of its colors and shades are the function of the entire world in the ten directions. No one can take it away, or throw a tile at it in the marketplace. Do not be concerned about falling or not falling into cause and effect in the six paths. Not ignoring cause and effect, from beginning to end, is the face of the bright pearl, is the eye of the bright pearl.

To think or not to think one hundred times about what the bright pearl is, or is not, is like gathering and binding weeds* [to trap yourself].* But when you clarify the body and mind as the bright pearl through the dharma words of Xuansha, you understand that mind is not the self.

Who is concerned if appearing and disappearing is the bright pearl or not? Even if you are concerned, that does not mean you are not the bright pearl. It is not something outside of the bright pearl that causes practice and thought. Therefore, your every step, forward or backward, in the demon's cave in the black mountain is just one bright pearl.

Presented to the assembly of the Kannon-dori Kosho Horin Monastery, Uji County, Yamashina Province, on the eighteenth day, the fourth month, the fourth year of the Katei Era [1238].

DRAGON SONG*

TOUZI,* GREAT MASTER CIJI of Shu Region, was once asked by a monk, "Is there a dragon* singing in a withered tree?*"

Touzi replied, "I say there is a lion roaring* in a skull.*"

Discussions about a withered tree and dead ash* [composure in stillness] are originally teachings outside the way. But the withered tree spoken of by those outside the way and that spoken of by buddha ancestors are far apart. Those outside the way talk about a withered tree, but they don't authentically know it; how can they hear the dragon singing? They think that a withered tree is a dead tree that does not grow leaves in spring.

The withered tree spoken of by buddha ancestors is the understanding of the ocean drying up.* The ocean drying up is the tree withering. The tree withering encounters spring.* The immovability of the tree is its witheredness. The mountain trees, ocean trees, and sky trees right now are all withered trees. That which sprouts buds is a dragon singing in a withered tree. Those who embrace it a hundred-fold, thousand-fold, and myriad-fold are descendants of the withered tree.

The form, characteristics, essence, and power of this witheredness are a withered stake spoken of by a buddha ancestor [Sushan Kuangren*]. It is beyond a withered stake. There are mountain valley trees, and fields-of-village trees. The mountain

59

valley trees are called pines and cypresses in the common world. The fields-of-village trees are called humans and devas in the common world. Those who depend on roots and spread leaves are called buddha ancestors. They all go back to the essence. This is to be studied. This is the tall dharma body* of a withered tree and the short dharma body* of a withered tree.

Without a withered tree there wouldn't be a dragon singing. Without a withered tree the dragon's singing wouldn't be smashed. "I have encountered spring many times but the mind has not changed" [a line by Damei Fachang*] is the dragon singing with complete witheredness. Although the dragon's singing does not conform with gong, shang, jue, zhi, yu [do, re, mi, fa, so], yet gong, shang, jue, zhi, yu are the before and after, two or three elements of the dragon's singing.

In this way, the monk's question *Is there a dragon singing in a withered tree?* emerges for the first time as a question for immeasurable eons. As for Touzi's response *I say there is a lion roaring in a skull*—what could hinder it? It keeps bending self and pushing other without ceasing. The skull covers the entire field.

Xiangyan,* Great Master Xideng of the Xiangyan Monastery, was once asked by a monk, "What is the way?"

Xiangyan said, "A dragon is singing in a withered tree."

The monk said, "I don't understand."

Xiangyan said, "An eyeball in the skull."

Later, a monk asked Shishuang,* "What is a dragon singing in a withered tree?"

Shishuang said, "Still it holds joy."

The monk asked, "What is the eyeball in the skull?"

Shishuang said, "Still it holds consciousness."

Later, a monk asked Caoshan,* "What is a dragon singing in a withered tree?"

Caoshan said, "The blood vein* does not get cut off."

The monk asked, "What is the eyeball in the skull?"

Caoshan said, "It does not dry up."

The monk said, "I wonder if anyone has heard it?"

Caoshan said, "In the entire world there is no one that has not heard it."

The monk said, "I wonder what kind of song the dragon sings?"

Caoshan said, "No one knows what kind of song the dragon sings. But all who hear it lose their lives.*"

The one who questions hearing and singing is not the one who sings the dragon song. The dragon song has its own melody. *In a withered tree* or *in a skull* is neither inside nor outside, neither self nor other. It is right now and a long time ago.

Still it holds joy is growing a horn on the head.* *Still it holds consciousness* is the skin dropping off completely.*

Caoshan's words *The blood vein does not get cut off,* are not hidden, turning the body in the word vein.* *It does not dry up,* means that the ocean's dryness never reaches to the bottom. Because the never-reaching is itself dryness, it is dryness beyond dryness.

To ask *if anyone has heard it* is like asking if there is anyone who has not got it. In regard to Caoshan's statement, *In the entire world there is no one that has not heard it,* you should ask further: "Never mind the fact that there is no one who has not heard it, where is the dragon's song at the time when no one in the entire world has heard it? Say it quickly, quickly!"

I wonder if anyone has heard it? Regarding this question, you should say, "The dragon song is howling and humming in muddy water,* exhaling through the nostrils.*"

No one knows what kind of song the dragon sings is to have a dragon in the song. *All who hear it lose their lives* is just to be longed for.

Now, the dragon songs of Xiangyan, Shishuang, and Caoshan come forth, forming clouds and forming water.* They go beyond saying or not saying eyes in the skull. This is thousand

and myriad tunes of the dragon song. *It still holds joy* is the croaking of frogs. *It still holds consciousness* is the singing of earthworms. Thus, the blood vein does not get cut off, a gourd* succeeding a gourd. As *it does not dry up* a pillar conceives a child; a lantern faces a lantern.

Presented to the assembly on the foot of Yamashi Peak on the twenty-fifth day, the twelfth month, the first year of the Kangen Era [1243].

GREAT ENLIGHTENMENT*

THE GREAT WAY OF THE BUDDHAS has been transmitted with intimate attention; the work of the ancestors has been unfolded evenly and broadly. Thus, great enlightenment is actualized and beyond-enlightenment is the decisive way. In this way, enlightenment is realized and fooled with; enlightenment disappears in the practice of letting go. This is the everyday activity of buddha ancestors. Enlightenment taken up activates the twelve hours* of the day. Enlightenment hurled away is activated by the twelve hours of the day. Furthermore, leaping beyond the mechanism of time, there is fooling with a mud ball and fooling with spirit.

Although it should be thoroughly understood that buddha ancestors are invariably actualized from great enlightenment, it is not that the entire experience of great enlightenment should be regarded as buddha ancestors, and it is not that the entire experience of buddha ancestors should be regarded as entire enlightenment. Buddha ancestors leap beyond the boundary of great enlightenment, and great enlightenment has a face that leaps further beyond buddha ancestors.

Now, human capacity is greatly varied. For example, there are those who already have understanding at birth. At birth, they are free from birth. That means they understand with the body at the beginning, middle, and end of birth. There are those who understand through study, ultimately understanding the self through practice. That means they practice with the body—the skin, flesh, bones, and marrow of study.

Besides those who have understanding at birth or through study, there are those who have understanding as buddhas. They go beyond the boundary of self and other, having no limit in this very place, and are not concerned with the notion of self and other. There are also those who understand without teachers. Although they do not rely upon teachers, sutras, self-nature, or form, and they do not turn the self around nor merge with others, nevertheless all things are revealed.

Among these types of people, don't regard one as sharp and another as dull. Various types of people, as they are, actualize various types of accomplishments. You should examine what sentient or insentient being is without understanding at birth. If one has understanding at birth, one has enlightenment at birth, realization at birth, and practice at birth. Therefore, the buddha ancestors who are already excellent tamers of beings are regarded as those who have enlightenment at birth. This is so because their birth has brought forth enlightenment. Indeed, this is enlightenment at birth that is filled with great enlightenment. This is the study of twirling enlightenment. Thus, one is greatly enlightened by twirling the three realms,* by twirling one hundred grasses,* by twirling the four great elements,* by twirling buddha ancestors, and by twirling the fundamental point. All these are further attaining great enlightenment by twirling great enlightenment. The very moment for this is just now.

Linji, Great Master Huizhao, said, "In the great nation of Tang China, if you look for a single person who is not enlightened, it is hard to find one."

This statement by Linji is the skin, flesh, bones, and marrow of the authentic stream that is not mistaken. *In the great nation of Tang China* means within the eyeball of self, which is not limited to the entire world or the dusty world. If you look for a single person who is not enlightened in just this, you cannot find one. The self of yesterday's self is not unenlightened. The self of today's other is not unenlightened. Between the past and present of a mountain-being and water-being, no one is unenlightened. Students of the way should study Linji's statement in this way without wasting time.

However, you should further study the heart of the work in the ancestral school. Now, addressing Linji you should ask, "If you only know that it is hard to find an unenlightened person and do not know that it is hard to find an enlightened one, it is not yet sufficient. It is impossible to say that you have thoroughly understood the fact that it is hard to find an unenlightened one. Even if it is hard to find an unenlightened one, have you not seen half a person who is not yet enlightened but has a serene face and magnificent composure?"

Thus, do not admit that the statement *In the great nation of Tang China, if you look for a single person who is not enlightened, it is hard to find one* expresses an ultimate understanding. Try to find two or three Tang Chinas within one person or half a person. Is it, or is it not, hard to find one? When you have the eye to see this, you can be regarded as a mature buddha ancestor.

Jingzhao Xiujing,* Great Master Baozhi, of Huayan Monastery in Jingzhao, was a dharma heir of Dongshan. Once a monk asked him, "What happens when a greatly enlightened person becomes deluded?"

Jingzhao said, "A broken mirror no longer reflects images. Fallen flowers hardly ever climb up the tree."

The monk's question is like a dharma talk to the assembly. Outside the assembly of the Huayan Monastery, this would not have been spoken. And one who was not a dharma heir of Dongshan could not have responded like this. Indeed, he was someone mature enough to sit on the seat of a buddha ancestor.

The so-called *greatly enlightened person* has not been enlightened from the beginning nor has received enlightenment from somewhere else. Great enlightenment is not something one encounters when one is old after having worked for a long time as an ordinary monk in a communal place. It does not emerge by pulling it out from oneself. Nevertheless, one is greatly enlightened.

Don't regard not being deluded as great enlightenment. Don't try to become deluded to obtain the seeds for great enlightenment. A greatly enlightened person is further greatly enlightened. A greatly deluded person is further greatly enlightened. Just as there is one who is greatly enlightened, there is a greatly enlightened buddha; greatly enlightened earth, water, fire, air, and emptiness; a greatly enlightened pillar and lantern. This is the meaning of *a greatly enlightened person* in the monk's question.

What happens when a greatly enlightened person becomes deluded? This is indeed a question to be asked. Jingzhao did not avoid it. This question has been admired in Zen monasteries as a meritorious work of a buddha ancestor. You should investigate it.

Is a greatly enlightened person who becomes deluded the same as an unenlightened person? When a greatly enlightened person becomes deluded, does the person use great enlightenment to create delusion? Does the person bring delusion from somewhere else and become deluded by covering the great enlightenment with delusion? Or, is it that a greatly enlightened person does not destroy great enlightenment but practices delusion? Or, is it that *a greatly enlightened person becomes deluded* means delusion brings forth another great enlightenment? You should study thoroughly in this way.

Is it that great enlightenment is a single hand, or is it that becoming deluded is a single hand? To inquire how a greatly enlightened person can become deluded should be the ultimate point of study. You should understand that there is great enlightenment that makes becoming deluded intimate.

Accordingly, it is not that recognizing the thief as one's own child is delusion, nor is it that recognizing one's own child as the thief is delusion. It is just that great enlightenment is to recognize the thief as the thief. Delusion is to recognize one's own child as one's own child. Adding a little to a lot is great enlightenment. Taking out a little from a little is delusion. Accordingly, look for a deluded person and encounter a greatly enlightened one just as you grasp the deluded one. Is the self right now delusion or not delusion? Examine this and bring it to yourself. This is called encountering a buddha ancestor.

Jingzhao said, *A broken mirror no longer reflects images. Fallen flowers hardly ever climb up the tree.* This teaching speaks of the moment when the mirror is broken. It is wrong to study the words *broken mirror* and compare the moment with the time when the mirror is not broken. It is a mistake to interpret Jingzhao's words to mean that a greatly enlightened person is no longer deluded as he neither reflects images nor climbs up the tree. This is not a study of the way as it is.

If what ordinary people think were right, you should ask, "What is the everyday activity of a greatly enlightened person?" They might say, "Can such a person still become deluded?" That is not how we should understand the dialogue between Jingzhao and the monk.

When the monk asked, *What happens when a greatly enlightened person becomes deluded?* he was asking about the very moment a greatly enlightened person becomes deluded. The very moment when these words are uttered, a broken mirror no longer reflects images and fallen flowers hardly ever climb up the tree. When fallen flowers are just fallen flowers, even if they get up to the top of a one-hundred-foot pole, they are still fallen flowers. When a broken mirror is just a broken mirror, whatever activities occur, they are merely broken pieces that no longer reflect images. Take up the teaching of the words *a broken mirror* and *fallen flowers* and study the moment when a greatly enlightened person becomes deluded.

Do not regard great enlightenment as becoming a buddha, or returning to the source and manifesting a buddha body. Do not regard becoming deluded as returning to be a sentient being. People with mistaken views talk about breaking great enlightenment and returning to be a sentient being. But Jingzhao was neither implying that great enlightenment gets broken or lost, nor that delusion appears. Do not think like those who have mistaken views.

Indeed, great enlightenment is limitless, delusion is limitless, and delusion does not hinder great enlightenment; take up threefold great enlightenment and turn it into a half-fold minor delusion. Thus, the Himalayas* are greatly enlightened to benefit the Himalayas. Wood and stone are greatly enlightened taking the forms of wood and stone. Buddhas' great enlightenment is greatly enlightened for the sake of sentient beings. Sentient beings' great enlightenment is greatly enlightened by buddhas' great enlightenment. This goes beyond before and after. Great enlightenment right at this moment is not self, not other. Great enlightenment does not come from somewhere else—the ditch is filled in and the stream is stopped up. Great enlightenment does not go away—stop following others. How? Follow all the way through.

Mihu* of Jingzhao sent a monk to ask Yangshan, "Do people nowadays pretend to have enlightenment?"

Yangshan said, "It's not that they are not enlightened, but how can they avoid falling into the secondary?"

The monk returned and reported this to Mihu, who then approved Yangshan.

The *nowadays* spoken of here is the right now of each of you. Even if you think of the past, present, and future millions of times, all time is this very moment, right now. Where you are is nothing but this very moment. Furthermore, an eyeball is this moment, a nostril* is this moment. Quietly investigate this question: *Do people nowadays pretend to have enlightenment?* Revive this question with your heart, revive this question with the top of your head.

These days shaven-headed monks in Song China vainly look for enlightenment, saying that enlightenment is the true goal, though they don't seem to be illuminated by the light of buddha ancestors. Because of laziness they miss the opportunity of studying with true teachers. They may not be able to attain liberation even if they were to encounter the emergence of authentic buddhas.

Mihu's question does not mean that there is no enlightenment, that there is enlightenment, or that enlightenment comes from somewhere else. This question asks whether or not people pretend to have enlightenment. It is like saying, "How are people nowadays enlightened?" If you speak of "achieving enlightenment," you may think that you don't usually have enlightenment. If you say, "Enlightenment comes," you may wonder where it comes from. If you say, "I have become enlightened," you may suppose that enlightenment has a beginning. Mihu did not speak that way. When he spoke of enlightenment, he simply asked about *pretend to have enlightenment.*

Yangshan's words *how can they avoid falling into the secondary* mean that the secondary is also enlightenment. *The secondary* is like saying "to become enlightened," "to get enlightenment," or "enlightenment has come." It means that "becoming" and "coming" are enlightenment.

It may look like Yangshan was cautious about falling into the secondary, and was denying a secondary enlightenment. But the secondary that becomes enlightenment is no other than the secondary that is true enlightenment. This being so, even the secondary, the hundredth, or the thousandth is enlightenment. It is not that the secondary is capped by the primary. Don't say that yesterday's self was the true self, but today's self is the secondary self. Don't say that enlightenment just now is other than enlightenment yesterday. It is not that enlightenment has begun this moment. Study in this way. Thus, great enlightenment is black, great enlightenment is white.

Abiding at the Konnon-dori Kosho Horin Moastery, I present this to the assembly on the twenty-seventh day, the first month of the third year of the Ninji Era [1242].

Staying at the ancient Yoshimine Temple, I revise and present this to the assembly of humans and devas on the twenty-seventh day, the first month of the second year of the Kangen Era [1243].

OCEAN MUDRA* SAMADHI

BUDDHAS AND ANCESTORS continuously maintain ocean mudra samadhi. While swimming in this samadhi, they expound, realize, and practice. Traveling through water includes journeying along the ocean bottom. This is called "coursing along the bottom of the deepest ocean."

This ocean differs from the sea of birth and death,* where buddhas guide drifting beings to the shore of liberation. Each buddha ancestor breaks through the bamboo node [intellectual thinking] and passes the barrier individually; this is done only through the power of the ocean mudra samadhi.

The Buddha said, "Elements come together and form this body. At the time of appearing, elements appear. At the time of disappearing, elements disappear. When elements appear, I do not say 'I' appear. When elements disappear, I do not say 'I' disappear. Past moments and future moments do not arise in sequence. Past elements and future elements are not in alignment. This is the meaning of ocean mudra samadhi."

Closely investigate these words by the Buddha. Attaining the way and entering realization does not necessarily require extensive learning or explanation. Anyone can attain the way through a simple verse of four lines. Even scholars of extensive knowledge can enter realization through a one-line verse. But these words by the Buddha are not about searching for original enlightenment* or gaining initial enlightenment.* Although buddhas and ancestors manifest original or initial enlightenment, original or initial enlightenment is not buddha ancestors.

At the very moment of the ocean mudra samadhi, elements come together and the Buddha's words *elements come together* are manifested. This is the moment when elements *form this body*.

This body is a coming together of elements. This body is not merely a coming together; it is elements coming together. A body formed in this way is described as *this body*.

The Buddha said, *At the time of appearing, elements appear*. This appearing does not leave any mark of appearing; therefore appearing does not come into one's perception or knowledge. Thus, the Buddha said, *I do not say 'I' appear*. It is not that there is someone else who perceives or thinks that he appears, it is just that you see into this directly, and you understand directly.

As the time [of ocean mudra samadhi] is not other than appearing, appearing is the arrival of time. What is it that appears? Appearing appears. Because appearing is time, appearing does not fail to fully manifest skin, flesh, bones, and marrow. As appearing is a coming together, appearing is this body, appearing is *'I' appear*, appearing is all elements coming together. What appears is not merely sound and form. All elements appear as *'I' appear* and as *I do not say 'I' appear*.

Not [to] say is not "not expressing," because expressing is not saying. The time of appearing [in ocean mudra samadhi] is when elements appear, which is not the same as the twelve hours of the day. "All elements" are the time of appearing, not the time when the three realms appear.

An ancient buddha said, "Fire appears all of a sudden."

Fire here means elements appear together but are not in sequence.

An ancient buddha said, "What about the moment when appearing and disappearing continue endlessly?"

Appearing and disappearing continue endlessly while self

appears and disappears. Reflect on the words *continue endlessly* and let them continue endlessly. Allow the moments of appearing and disappearing to continue and discontinue as the life stream of buddha ancestors.

The moment when appearing and disappearing continue endlessly is "What appears and disappears?" This means "With this body I awaken beings," "Now I manifest this body," "I expound dharma," "Past mind is inexhaustible," "You have attained my marrow,*" "You have attained my bones." This is "What appears and disappears?"

[The Buddha said,] *When elements disappear, I do not say 'I' disappear.* The moment when *I do not say 'I' disappear* is the moment when elements disappear. What disappears are elements disappearing. Although disappearing, they are elements. Because they are elements, they are not affected by delusion. Because they are not affected by delusion, they are not divided. This nondividedness* is all buddhas and ancestors. When Huineng said, "You are like this," what is not "you"? All past moments and all future moments are "you." When he said, "I am like this," what is not "I"? Past moments and future moments are all "I."

Disappearing has been magnificently expressed as countless hands and eyes* [of Avalokiteshvara Bodhisattva]. It is unsurpassable, boundless nirvana. It is called death, freedom from attachment, or an abiding place.

Hands and eyes are expressions of disappearing. Not saying "I" at the moment of appearing and not saying "I" at the moment of disappearing, appear together, but do not disappear at once. There are past elements that disappear and future elements that disappear. There are elements that are moments in the past and elements that are moments in the future. Being is past and future elements. Being is past and future moments. Things that are not sequential are being. Things that are not aligned are being.

To talk about things that are not sequential and not aligned explains eight or nine out of ten. To regard the four great elements and the five skandhas* as the hands and eyes of disappearing is to continue pursuing understanding. To see the four great elements and the five skandhas as the path of disappearing is going beyond, encountering reality. The entire body is hands and eyes, not lacking anything. The full range of the body is hands and eyes, not lacking anything. Disappearing is the activity of buddha ancestors.

Although the Buddha says *not in sequence* and *not aligned*, nevertheless, appearing arises in the beginning, middle, and end. This may be seen as officially not allowing a needle, but unofficially permitting carriages and horses to pass.*

In the beginning, middle, and end, disappearing is neither sequential nor aligned. Although elements appear *all of a sudden* where past elements disappeared, it is not that disappearing turns into appearing, but that elements appear. Because elements appear completely, they are neither sequential nor aligned. It does not mean that disappearings succeed disappearings or are aligned with disappearings. Disappearing is complete disappearing in the beginning, middle, and end. Disappearing meets disappearing, with nothing taken away; the entire mind knows there is disappearing.

Although elements disappear *all of a sudden* where past elements appeared, it is not that appearing turns into disappearing, but that elements disappear. Because elements disappear completely, they are neither sequential nor aligned.

Whether it is just appearing or just disappearing, in ocean mudra samadhi, all elements are as they are. It is not that there is no practice and realization, it is just that they are not divided. This is called ocean mudra samadhi.

Samadhi is actualization; it is expression. It is the night when a hand reaches back, groping for a pillow.* When the hand reaches back for a pillow at night, this groping is not limited to thousands and millions of eons, but it is [as the Buddha says in the *Lotus Sutra*], "I am always in the ocean expounding the *Wondrous Lotus Sutra*."

The Buddha said, *I do not say 'I' appear.* This means, *I am always in the ocean.* From his front the Buddha always teaches that "When one wave moves, thousands of waves follow." From the back he teaches the *Lotus Sutra,* expounding, "When thousands of waves move, one wave follows." Even if you cast a one-thousand-foot or a ten-thousand-foot fishing line, regrettably it only goes straight down. Both front and back spoken of here are *I am in the ocean.* They are just like the front and back of the head. Saying front and back of the head means placing one head on top of another.

It is not that there is a person *in the ocean.* The ocean of *I am in the ocean* is not an abode of people in the world. It is not where sages love to be. It is just "I am alone in the ocean." Thus, the Buddha said, *I am always in the ocean expounding.*

This ocean belongs to neither inside nor outside, nor in-between. It is just *I am always expounding the Wondrous Lotus Sutra.* The Buddha does not abide in the east, west, south, or north. The whole boat is empty; it returns full of moonlight. This return is a true place of settling. Who could call it stagnant water? It is actualized in the ultimate dimension of the buddha-dharma. This is called the mudra of water mudra.

It is the mudra of emptiness. It is the mudra of mud. The mudra of water is not necessarily the mudra of ocean. Going beyond is the mudra of ocean. This is called ocean mudra, water mudra, mud mudra, and mind mudra. By transmitting the mind mudra, you mudra water, you mudra mud, you mudra emptiness.

Caoshan, Great Master Yuanzheng, was asked by a monk, "From the scriptures we learn that an ocean does not retain corpses. What is the ocean?"

Caoshan said, "That which contains myriad things."

The monk said, "The ocean does not keep corpses. Why?"

Caoshan said, "Those who have stopped breathing do not remain as they are."

The monk said, "The ocean contains myriad things, but those who have stopped breathing do not remain as they are. Why?"

Caoshan said, "Myriad things stop breathing when they don't function any more."

Caoshan, a dharma brother of Yunju,* was right on the mark of Dongshan's teaching. *From the scriptures we learn* refers to the correct teaching of buddha ancestors. It is not the teaching of ordinary sages, nor is it a lesser teaching of the buddha-dharma.

The ocean that *does not retain corpses* is not open water, it is not enclosed sea, or even one of the Eight Seas.* This is not what the student asked Caoshan. The student understands what is not the ocean as the ocean, but also understands the ocean as the ocean.

A sea is not the ocean. The ocean is not necessarily an abyss of water with eight virtues* or nine trenches of salt water; the ocean is where all elements come together. It is not limited to deep water. This being so, the student's question *What is the ocean?* refers to an ocean that is not known by humans and devas. The one who asked this question wanted to shake up fixed views.

An ocean does not retain corpses is [as Puhua* said], "When brightness arises, meet it with brightness; when darkness arises, meet it with darkness." A corpse is as indestructible as ash, meaning [as Xiangyan Fachang said], "Through countless springs, there is no change of mind." A corpse such as this has not been seen before, therefore it is unknown.

Caoshan's words *That which contains myriad things* indicates the deep ocean. The point of his words is not about one thing that contains the myriad things but about just containing myriad things. He did not merely mean that the deep ocean contains myriad things, but that which contains myriad things is nothing other than the deep ocean.

Recognized or not, myriad things are just myriad things. Encountering the buddha face and the ancestor face is nothing other than fully recognizing myriad things as myriad things. Because myriad things are all-inclusive, you do not merely stand atop the highest peak or travel along the bottom of the deepest ocean.

Being all-inclusive is just like this; letting go is just like that. What is called the ocean of buddha nature or Vairochana's ocean storehouse, are just myriad things. Although the ocean surface is invisible, there is no doubt about the practice of swimming around.

Duofu* described a grove of bamboo as "one or two stalks are bent and three or four stalks are leaning." Although he referred to myriad things, why did he not say, "One thousand stalks, ten thousand stalks are bent"? Why did he not say "one thousand or ten thousand groves"? Do not forget that a grove of bamboo is like that. This is what is meant by Caoshan's words, *That which contains myriad things.*

The monk's statement, *Those who have stopped breathing do not remain as they are. Why?* appears to be a question, but it actually is an understanding of thusness. When doubt arises, just encounter doubt. In investigating thusness the monk said, *Those who have stopped breathing do not remain as they are. Why?* And, *The ocean does not retain corpses. Why?* This is the meaning of his words: *The ocean contains myriad things, but those who have stopped breathing do not remain as they are. Why?* You should know that containing does not allow things to remain as they are. Containing is not retaining. Even if myriad things were nothing but corpses, for ten thousand years the ocean would never retain them unchanged. The old monk, who does not remain the same, makes his move.

Caoshan's words, *The myriad things stop breathing when they don't function any more* mean that even if myriad things do or do not stop breathing, they do not remain as they are. Even if corpses are corpses, the practice of being one with myriad things should be able to contain them; the practice is all-containing. In the past and future of myriad things, there is a function that goes beyond not breathing. This is the blind leading the blind. The meaning of the blind leading the blind is that a blind one leads a blind one; blind ones lead blind ones. When blind ones lead blind ones,* all things are contained. Containing contains all things.

In the great way of going beyond, no endeavor is complete without being one with myriad things. This is ocean mudra samadhi.

Written at the Kannon-dori Kosho Horin Monastery on the twentieth day, the fourth month, the third year of the Ninji Era [1242].

AWESOME PRESENCE OF
ACTIVE BUDDHAS

BUDDHAS INVARIABLY PRACTICE complete awesome presence; thus, they are active buddhas. Active buddhas are neither reward-body* buddhas, nor incarnate-body* buddhas, neither self-manifested buddhas nor buddhas manifested from others. Active buddhas are neither originally enlightened, nor enlightened at some particular time, neither naturally enlightened, nor without enlightenment. Such buddhas can never compare with active buddhas.

Know that buddhas in the buddha way do not wait for awakening. Active buddhas alone fully experience the vital process on the path of going beyond buddha. This is something that self-manifested buddhas and the like have never dreamed of.

Because active buddhas manifest awesome presence in every situation, they bring forth awesome presence with their body. Thus, their transformative function flows out in their speech, reaching throughout time, space, buddhas, and activities. Without being an active buddha, you cannot be liberated from bondage to buddha and bondage to dharma, and you will be pulled into the cult of buddha-demons and dharma-demons.

"Bondage to buddha" means to be bound by the view that our perception and cognition of bodhi is actually bodhi. Experiencing such views even for a moment, you cannot expect to meet liberation, and you will remain vainly mistaken.

Seeing bodhi as nothing but bodhi may appear as a view that corresponds to bodhi. Who would imagine calling it a crooked view? But this is to tie yourself up without a rope. Becoming further and further bound up, the tree you are tied to does not topple, and the wisteria vine binding you does not wither. In vain you struggle inside a pit in the vicinity of buddha, without seeing it as a sickness of the dharma body* or as a trap of the reward body.*

Teachers of Buddhism, such as scholars of the sutras and treatises who listen to the buddha way from afar, say that "To arouse a view of dharma nature within dharma nature is no other than ignorance." These teachers talk about arousing a view of dharma nature without clarifying the bondage to dharma nature; they only accumulate the bondage of ignorance. They do not know about the bondage to dharma nature. Although this is regrettable, their awareness of the accumulation of the bondage of ignorance can be the seed for arousing bodhi mind.

Now, active buddhas are never bound by such ties. This being so, [it is said in the *Lotus Sutra*], "In the past I practiced the bodhisattva way, and have attained this long lifespan, still now unexhausted, covering vast numbers of years."

You should know that it is not that the lifespan of the bodhisattva has continued without end only until now or not that the lifespan of the Buddha has prevailed only in the past, but that what is called *vast numbers* is a total inclusive attainment. What is called *still now* is the total lifespan. Even if *in the past I practiced* is one solid piece of iron ten thousand miles long, it hurls away hundreds of years vertically and horizontally.

This being so, practice-realization is neither existence nor beyond existence. Practice-realization is not defiled. Although there are hundreds, thousands, and myriad [of practice-realizations] in a place where there is no buddha and no person, practice-realization does not defile active buddhas. Thus, there is no defilement in the practice-realization of active buddhas. It is not that there is no nondefilement* of practice-realization, but that this nondefilement is not nonexistent.

Huineng of Caoxi [the Sixth Ancestor] said [to Nanyue], "This very nondefilement is what is attentively maintained by all buddhas. You are also like this. I am also like this. All the ancestors in India are also like this."

Because *You are also like this*, there are all buddhas. Because *I am also like this*, there are all buddhas. Indeed, it is beyond me and beyond you. In this nondefilement *I* as I am, *attentively maintained by all buddhas*, is the awesome presence of an active buddha. *You* as you are, attentively maintained by all buddhas, is the awesome presence of an active buddha.

Because *I am also like this*, the teacher is excellent. Because you *are also like this*, the disciple is strong. The teacher's excellence and disciple's strength are the complete wisdom and practice of active buddhas. You should penetrate *what is attentively maintained by all buddhas*, as well as *I am also like this*, and *You are also like this*.

Even if this statement by the Old Buddha Caoxi were not about me, how could it not be about you? What is attentively maintained by active buddhas, and what is thoroughly mastered by active buddhas, is like this. Thus, we know practice and realization are not concerned with essence or forms, roots or branches. Although the everyday activities of active buddhas invariably allow buddhas to practice, active buddhas allow everyday activities to practice. This is to abandon your body for dharma, to abandon dharma for your body. This is to give up holding back your life, to hold on fully to your life. The awesome presence not only lets go of dharma for the sake of the dharma, but also lets go of the dharma for the sake of mind. Do not forget that this letting go is immeasurable.

Do not take up the buddha measure to measure and analyze the great way. The buddha measure is one corner, just like an open blossom. Do not hold out the mind measure to grope for and deliberate about the awesome presence. The mind measure is a single face, like the world. The measure of a single blade of grass is clearly the measure of the buddha ancestor mind—one blade that recognizes the whereabouts of active buddhas.

Even if you recognize that one mind measure encompasses innumerable buddha measures, when you try to measure the active buddhas' appearance in motion and stillness of their visage, it is undoubtedly beyond measure. Because their conduct is beyond measure, measuring does not hit the mark, is not useful, and cannot be gauged.

Now, there is another point for investigating the awesome presence of active buddhas. When "Buddha is no other than the self" comes thus, the awesome presence of *I also am like this* and *You also are like this* indicates "I alone know this." Yet, the dropping away of *The buddhas in the ten directions are also like this* is not merely a single avenue.

Accordingly, the Old Buddha [Hongzhi Zhengjue] said, "Reach over to grasp what's there, and bring its workings right here." When you take on sustaining this, all dharmas, bodies, actions, and buddhas are intimate to you. These actions, dharmas, bodies, and buddhas are simply covered in acceptance. Because they are simply covered in acceptance, through acceptance they are dropped off.

The covered eye is the radiance of a hundred grass-tips; do not be swayed [into thinking] that it does not see one dharma, does not see one thing. The covered eye reaches this dharma, and reaches that dharma. Throughout journeys, while taking on coming and going, or while leaving and entering by the same gate, nothing is hidden in the entire world. So the World-honored One's intimate language, intimate realization, intimate practice, and intimate entrustment are apparent.

Leaving the gate there is grass, entering the gate there is grass, but for myriad miles there is not a bit of grass. Such "entering" and "leaving" are not necessary. This grasping by entering does not wait for the letting go of leaving, but is just the apparition of blossoms in the sky.

Who would regard this apparition of blossoms in the sky as taking up a mistake and settling in with the mistake? Stepping forward misses, stepping backward misses, taking one step misses, taking two steps misses, and so there are mistakes upon mistakes.

Heaven and earth are far distant [due to our mistakes], and so the ultimate way is not difficult. You should thoroughly understand that in the awesome presence, and in the presence of awe, the great way is wide open. Know that upon emerging in birth, all emerge together on the way, and that upon entering death, all enter together on the way. From the head down to the tail, the awesome presence of rolling the pearl and of turning the jewel are manifested.

That which allows one corner of a buddha's awesome presence is the entire universe, the entire earth, as well as the entirety of birth and death, coming and going, of innumerable lands, and lotus blossoms. Each of these innumerable lands and lotus blossoms is one corner.

Many students think that "the entire universe" refers to this Southern Jambudvipa* Continent, or all the Four Continents.* Some may think of it as China or Japan. Regarding "the entire earth," there are those who think it is one billion worlds,* or simply a single province or prefecture. When you examine "the entire earth" or "the entire universe," you should investigate them three or five times without stopping, even though you already see them as vast.

Understanding these words [about the entire universe] is going beyond buddhas and ancestors by seeing the extremely large as small and the extremely small as large. Although this seems like denying that there is any such thing as large or small, this [understanding] is the awesome presence of active buddhas.

Understand that the awesome presence of the entire universe, the awesome presence of the entire earth, as revealed by buddhas and ancestors, is the unhidden inclusive world. This is not only the unhidden inclusive world, but also the awesome presence within a single active buddha.

In expounding the buddha way, womb birth and transformation birth are usually mentioned, but not moisture birth and egg birth. Furthermore, it has not even been dreamed that there could be births other than these four types.* Even further, has it been seen, heard, or realized that there are four types of birth* beyond the four types of birth? In the great way of buddhas and ancestors, it has been intimately and explicitly transmitted that there are four types of birth beyond [the usual understanding of] these four types of birth. What group of people has not heard, known, or clarified this understanding?

As these four types of birth are already known, how many types of death are there? Are there four types of death for the four types of birth, or are there two or three types of death? Are there five or six, one thousand, or ten thousand deaths? To have even a little doubt about this point is part of the inquiry.

Now consider whether there are beings among four types of beings who only have birth without death. Are there any beings who only transmit death, and do not transmit birth? You should study whether or not there are beings who have birth alone or death without birth.

There are people who hear the phrase "no birth," but do not clarify it, ignoring their body-and-mind endeavor. This is extreme foolishness. They should be called beasts who lack the capacity for faith, or for understanding dharma, or for sudden or gradual awakening. How is this so? Even though they hear the words "no birth," they neglect to question the meaning. And they do not ask further about no buddha, no way, no mind, no extinction, no no birth, no phenomenal world, no dharma nature, or no death. They are like oxen and horses who vainly think only of water and grass.

You should know that birth-and-death is the activity of the buddha way; birth-and-death is the furnishings of the buddha house. It is utilized when it needs to be utilized; it is fully clarified when it is clarified. Accordingly, all buddhas are clear about the implements of birth-and-death, and fully achieve their utilization. How can those who are ignorant of this realm of birth and death be called a person, or someone who has completed birth, or accomplished death? Do not believe that you are sunk in birth and death, or even think that you exist in birth and death. Do not blindly believe, nor misunderstand, nor disregard birth and death as merely birth and death.

Some people say that buddhas only appear in the human realm, and think that buddhas do not appear in other realms or worlds. If that were true, all realms would have been human realms when the Buddha was alive. This is like saying that human buddhas alone are venerable ones. However, there must be buddhas in the deva realm as well as buddhas in the buddha realm. Those who think that buddhas appear only in the human realm have not yet entered the inner chamber of buddha ancestors.

An ancestor said, "Shakyamuni Buddha received transmission of the true dharma from Kashyapa Buddha,* went to Tushita Heaven* to teach, and still abides there."

Indeed, you should know that Shakyamuni of the human realm spread the teaching through his manifestation of pari-nir-vana,* but Shakyamuni in the heavenly realm still abides there, teaching devas. Students should know that Shakyamuni of the human realm reveals infinitely varied expressions, actions, and teachings, auspiciously illuminating one corner of the human realm. It is foolish not to notice that Shakyamuni in the heavenly realm teaches in far more varied ways, in one thousand styles, in ten thousand gates.

The essential meaning of the great way, transmitted correctly from buddha to buddha, goes beyond cutting off, and drops away what is beginningless and endless. It has been correctly transmitted only in the buddha way. This merit has never been known or heard of by other beings.

Where active buddhas teach, there are beings that are not limited to the four types of birth. There are realms not limited to heavenly beings, humans, or the phenomenal world. When you look into the awesome presence of active buddhas, do not use the eyes of heavenly beings or humans. Do not use the deluded thinking of heavenly beings or humans. Do not try to analyze it using human or heavenly faculties. Even bodhisattvas of the ten stages and three classes* have not clarified this, so how could the analytical thinking of humans and devas reach it? When human calculation is small, knowledge is small. When a lifespan is fleeting, thinking is fleeting. Then, how is it possible to make calculations about the awesome presence of active buddhas?

This being so, do not accept as children of the Buddha any group of those who regards mere human views as the buddha-dharma, or who limits buddha-dharma to human dharmas. Such people are merely sentient beings conditioned by karma* who have not yet heard the dharma or practiced the way with body and mind. Neither are their life, death, views, and learning are in accord with dharma, nor are their walking, standing, sitting, or lying down. Such kinds of beings have not been nurtured or benefited by dharma.

Active buddhas hold on to neither fundamental enlightenment* nor acquired enlightenment,* and neither possess nor do not possess enlightenment—this is true indeed. Worldly people carry on deliberations about thinking and not thinking, having enlightenment or not having enlightenment, and fundamental or acquired enlightenment. These are merely worldly peoples' categories, but this is not what has been transmitted from buddha to buddha. The thinking of worldly people and the thinking of buddhas are completely different, and cannot be compared. The fundamental enlightenment discussed by worldly people and the fundamental enlightenment actualized by buddhas are as far apart from each other as heaven and earth; they are beyond comparison. Even the deliberations of bodhisattvas of the ten stages or three classes do not match the expressions of buddhas. How can worldly people, vainly counting grains of sand,* make accurate assessments?

Nevertheless, there are many people who merely agree to the crooked, inverted views of worldly people or of those outside the way, and then mistakenly regard such views as the realm of buddhas. Buddhas say that the unwholesome roots of such people are deep and heavy, and they are to be pitied. However endless the unwholesome roots of such people may be, that is their burden. For now, look into this and release it. Grasping such obstructions and involving yourself with them is not a good direction to pursue.

The awesome presence of active buddhas right now is beyond obstruction. Totally encompassed by buddhas, active buddhas are free from obstruction as they penetrate the vital path of being splattered by mud and soaked in water.* Active buddhas transform devas in the heavenly realm, and transform humans in the human realm. This is the power of opening blossoms and the power of the world arising. There has never been a gap in active buddhas' transformative work.

This being so, there is complete dropping of self and other; there is the total independence of coming and going. Immediately going to and coming from Tushita Heaven, this is immediately Tushita Heaven. Immediately going to and coming from blissful ease, this is immediately blissful ease. This is immediate and complete dropping of Tushita Heaven, and this is immediate and complete dropping of blissful ease. This is the immediate crushing of blissful ease in Tushita Heaven into a hundred pieces. This is no other than the immediate grasping and letting go of blissful ease in Tushita Heaven. This is swallowing up everything in one gulp.

Know that this blissful ease in Tushita Heaven is no other than transmigration, coming and going, within heavenly halls and the Pure Land. Because this blissful ease is the practice of coming and going, one practices equally in heavenly halls and the Pure Land.

Because this is great enlightenment, it is equally great enlightenment [within heavenly halls and the Pure Land]. In great delusion, it is equally great delusion. This is simply the toes wiggling in the sandals of active buddhas. Sometimes, it is the sound of a fart or the smell of shit throughout the single path [of active buddhas]. This is smelled with the nostrils, and heard with ears, body, and practice. There is further a moment of attaining "my skin, flesh, bones, and marrow." Moreover, there is no practice attained from others.

In regard to freely penetrating the great way that completes birth and masters death, there is an ancient statement: "A great sage surrenders birth and death to the mind, surrenders birth and death to the body, surrenders birth and death to the way, surrenders birth and death to birth and death." As this teaching is actualized without limitation in the past and present, the awesome presence of active buddhas is thoroughly practiced immediately.

The teaching of birth and death, body and mind, is the circle of the way and is actualized at once. Thoroughly practicing, thoroughly clarifying, it is not forced. It is just like recognizing the shadow of deluded thought and turning the light to shine within. The clarity of clarity beyond clarity prevails in the activity of buddhas. This is totally surrendering to practice.

To understand the principle of total surrendering, you should thoroughly investigate mind. In the steadfastness of thorough investigation, all phenomena are the unadorned clarity of mind. You know and understand that the three realms of desire, form, and formlessness are merely elaborate divisions of mind. Although your knowing and understanding are part of all phenomena, you actualize the home village of the self. This is no other than your everyday activity.

This being so, the continuous effort to grasp the point in phrases and to seek eloquence beyond words is to take hold beyond taking hold, and to let go beyond letting go.

In this endeavor, what is birth? What is death? What are body and mind? What are giving and taking? What are surrendering and rejecting? Is there no encounter while entering and exiting the same gate? Is there hiding the body but exposing the horns within a single move? Do we understand from great deliberation, or know with considerate intention? Is this endeavor one bright pearl or the entire treasury of the sutras? Is it a single monk's staff, or a single layer of the face? Does this occur thirty years later, or in myriad years within one moment? Examine this in detail, and make a detailed study of this examination. In this detailed examination, hear sounds with your entire eye and see colors with your entire ear.

Further, opening the single eye of a monk is to go beyond phenomena before one's eyes, to go beyond objects before one's eyes. There is the composure of smiling and winking. This is the moment of the awesome presence of an active buddha. Not pulled by things or pulling things, not creating or producing causal conditions, not original nature or dharma nature, not abiding in one's dharma position, not original being, and not merely accepting any of these as suchness—this is simply the awesome presence of an active buddha.

This being so, fluctuating circumstances of being phenomena, or of being the body, are left to the mind. For now, the awesome presence of dropping off birth and dropping off death is solely surrendered to buddha. Thus, there is an understanding: "All things are mind only, and the three realms are mind only." Further, in an expression that goes beyond, there is a statement that "mind only" is called "walls and pebbles." Where there is no mind only, there are no walls and pebbles.

The point is that the awesome presence of active buddhas is entrusted to mind, is entrusted to things, being phenomena, being the body. This awesome presence cannot be reached through the notions of acquired enlightenment or fundamental enlightenment. Furthermore, how can it be reached by those outside the way, by those in the Two Vehicles, or by bodhisattvas in the three classes or the ten stages?

This awesome presence is simply not comprehended by any person, and is beyond comprehension on any level. However lively it may be, each branch is just as it is. Is it one long piece of iron? Is it both ends of a worm moving? One long piece of iron is neither long nor short; both ends moving are neither self nor other.

When the power of unrolling the matter and hurling insightful flashes is put into practice, the awesomeness encompasses all things, and the eye is exalted throughout the entire world. There is illumination that is not hindered by taking in or letting go. It is the monks' hall,* the buddha hall, the kitchen, or the monastery gate. Further, there is illumination that does not take in or let go. It is also the monks' hall, the buddha hall, the kitchen, or the monastery gate.

Moreover, there is an eye that penetrates the ten directions, and receives the entire earth. This eye is in front of the mind, and behind the mind. Such eye, ear, nose, tongue, body, and mind have the dazzling power of illumination. Thus, there are buddhas in the past, present, and future who maintain not knowing, and there are cats and white oxen who launch the insightful response of already knowing. This is grabbing the ox's nose and having an eye. This expresses the dharma of active buddhas and allows the dharma of active buddhas.

Xuefeng*, Great Master Zhenjue, said to the assembly, "Buddhas in the past, present, and future abide in flames and turn the great dharma wheel."

Xuansha*, Great Master Zhongyi, said in response, "As flames expound dharma to all buddhas in the past, present, and future, all buddhas remain standing and listen."

Keqin,* Zen Master Yuanwu, later commented on their words: "One says the monkey is white; the other says it is black. They hurl insightful flashes at each other; spirits emerge and demons vanish. Blazing flames in the spreading sky are buddhas expounding dharma; the spreading sky in blazing flames is dharma expounding buddhas. Amid the winds, these two masters cut apart the tangle of twining vines and with a single statement crush Vimalakirti* in his silence."

Now, buddhas in the past, present, and future means all buddhas. Active buddhas are all buddhas in the past, present, and future. All buddhas in the ten directions are none other than these buddhas in the three times.* Expounding fully, buddhas speak like this throughout the past, present, and future. If you want to inquire about active buddhas, they are exactly the buddhas in the past, present, and future. With or without knowing, they are invariably active buddhas as all buddhas in the three times.

This being so, the three ancient buddhas—Xuefeng, Xuansha, and Keqin—spoke like this to express their understanding of buddhas in the three times.

You should study the meaning of Xuefeng's statement: *Buddhas in the past, present, and future abide in flames and turn the great dharma wheel.* The practice place of buddhas in the three times turning the dharma wheel is invariably inside flames. Inside flames is always buddhas' place of practice. Teachers of sutras and commentaries have never heard this, and those outside the way, or in the Two Lesser Vehicles,* cannot know it. Know that the flames around all buddhas are not the same as the flames of other beings. Shed light on whether or not other beings are within flames.

Study how buddhas in the three times transform beings within flames. When they abide within flames, are the flames and buddhas intimate or are they separate? Are the buddhas and their surroundings integrated or are they independent? Are they of one piece or divided?

In turning the great dharma wheel, there is turning the self, turning insightful flashes. This is unrolling the matter and hurling insightful flashes, turning dharma and dharma turning. This is called turning the dharma wheel. Even if the entire great earth is entirely in flames, there must be the dharma wheel turning the flame wheel, the dharma wheel turning all buddhas, the dharma wheel turning the dharma wheel, and the dharma wheel turning past, present, and future. This being so, flames are the great practice place of all buddhas turning the dharma wheel. If you try to assess this with the measurements of realms, time, human capacity, or ordinary or sacred, you cannot hit the mark. Because it cannot be assessed by these calculations, all buddhas in the three times abide in flames and turn the great dharma wheel. As they are called all buddhas in the three times, they go beyond these measurements. Because it is the practice place of buddhas in the three times turning the dharma wheel, there are flames. Because there are flames, it is the practice place of all buddhas.

Xuansha said, *As flames expound dharma to all buddhas in the past, present, and future, all buddhas remain standing and listen.* You may hear this statement and say that Xuansha's words are more of a complete utterance than Xuefeng's words, but it is not necessarily so. Know that Xuefeng's statement is different from Xuansha's. That is, Xuefeng speaks about the place where all buddhas in the three times turning the great dharma wheel, while Xuansha speaks about all buddhas in the three times listening to the dharma.

Xuefeng's statement is indeed about turning the dharma, but he does not actually discuss listening or not listening to dharma at the place of turning dharma. Thus, it does not sound like turning the dharma is always listening to the dharma. Moreover, Xuefeng in his teaching did not say that buddhas in the three times expound dharma for the sake of flames. Nor did he say that buddhas in the three times turn the great dharma wheel for the sake of the buddhas in the three times, nor that flames turn the great dharma wheel for the sake of the flames. Is there any difference between the words, *turning the dharma wheel*, and *turning the great dharma wheel?** Turning the dharma wheel is not limited to expounding the dharma. Isn't expounding the dharma necessarily for the sake of others? Thus, it is not that the words of Xuefeng have not exhausted the meaning of the words that he should have said.

Definitely you should study in detail Xuefeng's words *abiding in flames and turning the great dharma wheel.* Don't be confused by Xuansha's words.

Penetrating Xuefeng's statement awesomely presents the awesome presence of buddhas. The flames that contain buddhas in the three times prevail not only in one or two limitless phenomenal worlds, and do not merely fill one or two particles of dust. In attempting to discern the great dharma wheel's turning, do not measure it as large or small, wide or narrow. Turning the great dharma wheel is neither for the self nor for others, neither for expounding nor for listening.

Xuansha said, "As flames expound dharma to all buddhas in the past, present, and future, all buddhas remain standing and listen." Although he said flames expound dharma to the buddhas in the three times, he did not say that flames turn the dharma wheel. Furthermore, he did not say that buddhas in the three times turn the dharma wheel. Although all buddhas in the three times remain standing and listening, how can the flames turn the dharma wheel of the buddhas in the three times? Do the flames that expound dharma for the buddhas in the three times also turn the great dharma wheel or not? Xuansha did not say that turning the dharma wheel occurs at this moment. He did not say that the dharma wheel does not turn. However, it might be supposed that Xuansha carelessly interpreted the turning of the dharma wheel as expounding the dharma wheel. If so, he did not yet comprehend the statement of Xuefeng.

Xuansha knew that when flames expound dharma for buddhas in the three times, buddhas all remain standing and listen to the dharma. However, he did not realize that where the flames turn the dharma wheel, flames remain standing and listen to the dharma. He did not say that where flames turn the dharma wheel, flames altogether turn the dharma wheel. All buddhas of the three times listening to the dharma is the dharma of all buddhas, which is not dependent on others. Do not consider the flames as dharma, as buddha, or even as flames. Indeed, do not ignore the statements of this master and his disciple. This is to say that not only are they red-bearded barbarians, but that they are barbarians with red beards.

Although Xuansha's words are like this, there is something you should study with great effort. Without regard to the limited views of the Great Vehicle or Lesser Vehicles held by teachers of sutras and treatises, just study the true characteristics that have been correctly transmitted from buddha to buddha, ancestor to ancestor.

Buddhas of the three times listen to the dharma. This is not limited to the views of the Great or Lesser Vehicles. Teachers of sutras and treatises only know that buddhas expound dharma in response to the readiness of those who hear it. But they do not say that buddhas listen to the dharma, that buddhas practice, and that buddhas accomplish buddhahood. Regarding Xuansha's words, *All buddhas in the past, present, and future remain standing and listen to the dharma*, this is the quality of buddhas' listening. Do not regard the capacity to expound the dharma as superior, and the capacity to listen to the dharma as inferior. If those who speak are venerable, those who listen are venerable as well.

Shakyamuni Buddha said, "To expound this *Lotus Sutra* is to see me. To expound it for the sake of even one person is difficult."

Thus, being able to expound the dharma is to see Shakyamuni Buddha, because *to see me* is itself Shakyamuni Buddha.

The Buddha also said, "After I pass away, to listen to and to accept this sutra, and to inquire into its meaning will be quite difficult."

Know that it is equally difficult to listen to and accept this sutra. Expounding and listening are not a matter of superior or inferior. Even if those who remain standing and listening are the most venerable buddhas, nevertheless they remain and listen to dharma, because all buddhas of the three times remain and listen to dharma. As the fruit of buddhahood is already present, they do not listen to dharma to achieve buddhahood; as [Xuansha] indicated, they are already buddhas of the three times.

Know that buddhas in the three times are buddhas who remain and listen to the dharma expounded by flames. The transformative function of this single phrase cannot be traced in a linear manner. If you try to trace it, the arrowhead and the shaft will crush each other. Flames definitely expound dharma for buddhas of the three times. With bits and pieces of red heart,* an iron tree blossoms and the world becomes fragrant. Let me ask: When buddhas remain standing and listen to the flames expound dharma, ultimately what is it that is actualized? This is wisdom surpassing the master, wisdom equaling the master. Further, there are buddhas in the three times investigating the inner sanctum of master and disciple.

Keqin's words *the monkey is white* do not conflict with the other monkey being black. Thus, Xuefeng and Xuansha hurl insightful flashes at each other as spirits emerge and demons vanish. Although there is a path that Xuefeng travels together with Xuansha, yet does not enter together with Xuansha, is it the case that the flames are all buddhas, or that all buddhas are the flames? Xuansha's mind interchanges black and white, emerging and vanishing like spirits and demons, while Xuefeng's voice and form do not remain in the realm of black and white. Further, see that Xuansha's statement is just right, beyond just right; and Xuefeng's statement takes it up, and releases it.

Keqin has a statement that is not the same as Xuansha's and not the same as Xuefeng's: *Blazing flames in the spreading sky are buddhas expounding dharma; the spreading sky in blazing flames is dharma expounding buddhas.* This statement has been truly illuminating for those who have studied since that time. Even if you do not notice the blazing flames, if you are covered by the spreading sky, you have your share and others have theirs. Wherever the entire sky covers you, there are always blazing flames. Even though you dislike these blazing flames and look somewhere else, how could it be otherwise?

Rejoice! Although your skin bag was born far from the sages, and although this moment is distant from the sages, you have encountered the transforming guidance of the spreading sky that can still be heard. Although we have heard the statement *buddhas expounding dharma*, how many layers of ignorance we have suffered from because of not having heard the statement *dharma expounding buddhas*! Accordingly, it is simply that all buddhas in the three times are expounded by dharma throughout the three times, and all dharmas in the three times are expounded by buddhas throughout the three times.

It is the spreading sky alone that cuts apart the tangle of twining vines amid the winds. A single statement crushes both Vimalakirti and not Vimalakirti, and nothing remains.

Thus, dharma expounds buddha, dharma practices buddha, dharma verifies buddha. Buddha expounds dharma, buddha practices buddha, buddha makes buddha. This is all the awesome presence of active buddhas. Throughout heaven and earth, throughout past and present, what they have attained is not insignificant, what they have clarified is not to be utilized casually.

Written in the middle of the tenth month, the second year of the Ninji Era [1241], at the Kannon-dori Horin Monastery by Monk Dogen.

ZAZEN IN COMMUNITY

REGULATIONS FOR THE
AUXILIARY CLOUD HALL*

At the Kannon-dori Kosho Gokoku Monastery

THOSE WHO HAVE WAY-SEEKING MIND and wish to abandon fame and fortune should enter. Those who are halfhearted and lack sincerity should not enter. If the entry is a mistake, after some consideration one may be asked to leave.

When the way-seeking mind is aroused inwardly, there is immediate freedom from fame and gain. In the vastness of a billion worlds, true heirs of dharma are rare. In spite of the long history of our country, you should make the present moment the true source, having compassion for later generations by giving emphasis to the present.

The assembly of practitioners in the hall should blend like milk and water to support the activity of the way. Although now for some period you are guest and host,* later you will be buddha ancestors equally throughout time. Therefore, you should not forget the feeling of gratitude. It is rare to meet one another and to practice what is rare to practice. This is called the body and mind of buddha-dharma. You will certainly become a buddha ancestor.

Having left your home and birthplace, now you depend on clouds and you depend on water. The support to you and your practice given by this assembly of practitioners surpasses that which was given by your father and mother. Your father and mother are temporarily close to you in birth and death, but this assembly of practitioners is your companion in the way of enlightenment for all time.

Do not look for a chance to go out. But if necessary, going out is permitted once a month. People in the past lived in the remote mountains and practiced far away in the forests. Not only were they free of nearly all worldly affairs, but they also abandoned all relationships. You should learn the heart of their covering brilliance and obscuring traces. Now is the time for the fire on your head to be wiped out. Is it not sad if you waste this time, concerning yourself with secular affairs? The impermanent is unreliable. No one knows where and when this dewlike existence will drop from the grass. Not recognizing impermanence is truly regrettable.

Do not read books in the hall, even Zen texts, and do not bring in personal correspondence. In the hall you should endeavor in the way of realizing the great matter. When facing the bright window, you should illuminate the mind with the authentic teaching. Do not waste a moment. Concentrate in your effort.

You should always inform the director of the hall where you are going to be, day or night. Do not play around according to your own impulses; your actions affect the discipline of the entire assembly. Who knows, this may be the last day of your life. It would be truly regrettable to die while indulging in pleasures.

Do not be concerned with the faults of others. Do not see others' faults with a hateful mind. There is an old saying that if you stop seeing others' faults, then naturally seniors are venerated and juniors are revered. Do not imitate others' faults; just cultivate virtue. The Buddha prohibited unwholesome actions but did not tell us to despise those who practice unwholesome actions.

When carrying out either important matters or trifles, you should always consult with the director of the hall. Those who do things without consulting with the director of the hall should leave. If you neglect the formality of guest and host, you can understand neither the true nor the phenomenal.

Inside or near the hall, do not put your heads together and talk loudly. The director should prohibit this.

Do not do chanting circumambulation in the hall.

Do not hold or carry beads* in the hall. Do not enter or leave with your hands hanging down.

Do not chant the names of buddhas or sutras in the hall. However, this is permitted when supporters request sutra chanting on a particular occasion.

Do not spit, blow your nose, or laugh loudly. You should be sobered by the fact that the work of the way is not yet thoroughly mastered. You should regret the subtle passage of time that is eating away this opportunity for practice of the way. Then, you may have the sense of being a fish in a small puddle.

Those assembled in the hall should not wear brocade but rather things like paper robes. Those who understood the way in the past were all like this.

Do not enter the hall intoxicated with wine. If you do so by accident, you should make formal repentance. Do not bring wine into the hall. Do not enter the hall smelling of onions.

Quarreling persons should go out of the hall, because it hinders not only their own work in the way but also that of others.

Those who see such quarreling and do not stop it are equally at fault.

Those who do not follow the admonitions of the hall should be removed. Those who are amused by or in sympathy with such practitioners are also at fault.

Do not show monks or laypeople around the hall, as this may disturb the practitioners. Do not speak loudly with guests near the hall. And do not talk about practice in a self-praising way, in order to get offerings. However, those who have a long-standing intention to practice or those who are on pilgrimage may be allowed inside. In such cases, you should always consult the director of the hall beforehand.

You should practice zazen in this hall just as in the monks' hall. Never neglect early morning zazen or the evening practice instruction period.

At mealtime, those who drop monk's bowls or utensils on the floor should be fined according to the regulations of the monastery.

The admonitions of buddha ancestors should always be followed. The pure guidelines of the monastery are to be inscribed on your bones and mind.

You should wish to be serenely composed for your entire life and to practice the way free of expectations.

These regulations are body and mind of the ancient buddhas. Respect and follow them.

Written on the twenty-fifth day, the fourth month, the first year of the En'o Era [1239].

GUIDELINES FOR
PRACTICE OF THE WAY

BUDDHAS AND ANCESTORS ENDEAVOR IN THE WAY without veering off. Where there are guidelines, endeavor in the way arises. Where there are no guidelines, endeavor in the way does not arise. This being so, when everyone sits, you sit. When everyone lies down, you lie down. Be one with everyone both in motion and in stillness. Do not leave the monastery in death or in birth. To be conspicuous in the community is not beneficial. To contradict the assembly is not appropriate. This is the skin, flesh, bones, and marrow of buddha ancestors. This is dropping off body and mind of the self. Thus, it is practice-realization beyond actualization since before the Empty Eon.* This is the fundamental point before the first signs appear. It does not await great enlightenment.

For evening zazen, put on the kashaya upon hearing the sound of the sunset bell, enter the monks' hall, and sit at your assigned place. The abbot sits in the dharma chair facing the enshrined image of the Sacred Monk* on the central altar. The head monk* sits facing out while the assembly of practitioners sit facing the wall. While the abbot sits, a low bench is set up outside the screen behind his dharma chair for the attendant monk or the attendant worker to sit by the abbot.

For zazen, the abbot enters from the north side [right side] of the front [east] entrance. He proceeds to the front of the Sacred Monk image, offers incense, and makes a standing bow.* He then holds his hands in shashu,* does a greeting circuit* to the practitioners in the hall, goes back to the Sacred Monk, and does a standing bow. He goes to his dharma chair, bows, turns around, bows to the Sacred Monk, tucks his sleeves under his arms, and sits on his chair. He takes off his sandals, lifts his legs, and sits in a lotus position.

The attendant monk or the attendant worker sits at the south side of the main entrance while the abbot does a greeting circuit. After the abbot is seated, the attendant monks go to their assigned seats, make greeting bows to the Sacred Monk, and quietly sit on the low chairs. One of them carries the abbot's small incense container.

In case the abbot wants to sleep overnight in the monks' hall, a special platform is set up next to the head monk's seat closer to the center. In the morning the abbot sits in the dharma chair for zazen.

For the late evening zazen, practitioners do not wear the kashaya. The abbot's kashaya is hung on the dharma chair during zazen. This is customary.

The abbot decides when to end zazen. It can be after the first-fifth, second-fifth, or third-fifth of the second, or third night period.* When the han* is struck to signal the end of zazen, practitioners bow in gassho,* fold the kashaya, put it in the wrapping cloth, and set it on the cabinet near the seat. The abbot, keeping his kashaya on, gets up from the dharma chair, goes to the Sacred Monk, does a standing bow, and leaves by way of the north side of the front entrance.

The attendants leave the monks' hall before the abbot and wait for him. One of them raises the screen and clears the way for him. This is also done when the abbot enters the monks' hall. If the abbot wants to sleep in the monks' hall, one or more attendants stay at the low bench behind the dharma chair. The

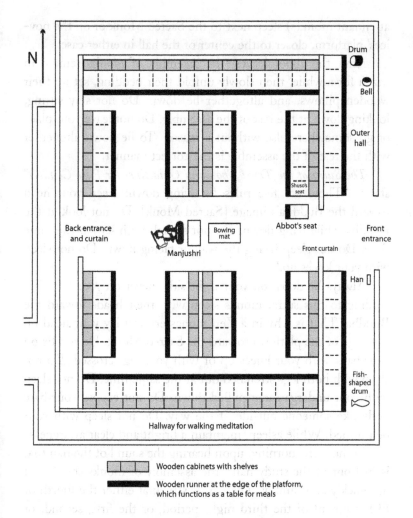

N

Drum

Bell

Outer
hall

Shuso's
seat

Abbot's seat

Front
entrance

Back entrance
and curtain

Bowing
mat

Manjushri

Front curtain

Han

Fish-
shaped
drum

Hallway for walking meditation

Wooden cabinets with shelves

Wooden runner at the edge of the platform,
which functions as a table for meals

Monks' hall. A presumed floor plan at the Daibutsu/Eihei Monastery during Dogen's time. Reconstructed from the current floor plan at the Eihei Monastery, drawn by Shohaku Okumura (Dogen's Pure Standards for the Zen Community).

attendant monk(s) sleep next to the Sacred Monk or on the novices' platform, closer to the center of the hall in either case.

After the abbot leaves, the assembly of monks remain in zazen for a while, then slowly unfold their bedding, set up their wooden pillows, and altogether lie down. Do not stay sitting, looking down at the rest of the assembly. Do not leave your place or go somewhere else without a reason. To lie down altogether with the rest of the assembly is the correct manner.

The Sutra of the Three Thousand Guidelines for Pure Conduct* states: "There are five rules for lying down: Keep your head toward the Buddha's image [Sacred Monk]. Do not look at the Buddha while lying down. Do not stretch both legs at the same time. Do not sleep facing the wall or facing down. Do not sleep with your knees up."

Always lie down on your right side, never on your left. According to this sutra, monks sleep with their heads toward the Buddha. That is why in a Zen monastery you lay your head on the edge of the platform toward the Sacred Monk. Do not lie on your back with your knees up or with your legs crossed. Do not sleep with both legs stretched out at the same time. Do not sleep with your undergarment pulled down. Do not expose your bare body like someone outside of the way. Do not sleep with your belt untied. While asleep, maintain a bright and clear awareness.

In the early morning, upon hearing the sound of the han that is in front of the study hall,* the assembly of monks should get up quickly and nimbly. The han is struck at either the fourth or fifth segment of the third night period, or the first, second, or third segment of the fourth night period. The han is struck in accordance with the abbot's instruction.

Do not get up in a rough manner or be rude to the assembly by remaining in bed. Quietly pick up your wooden pillow, place it in front of the cabinet for bedding,* without being noisy and annoying those around you.

Settling in your place, cover yourself with the bedding quilt and sit zazen for a short period on the cushion. Make an effort to refrain from closing your eyes. If you close your eyes, you may doze off. If you keep them open, fresh air brushes them, making it easier to stay awake. Be aware that life is impermanent and fleeting and that your practice of the way has not yet matured. Do not move your body, yawn, sigh, or flap your sleeves drawing attention to yourself. Always maintain a respectful attitude toward the assembly of fellow practitioners; do not take them lightly. Do not cover your head with the bedding. If you notice sleepiness, take off the bedding and continue sitting with a lighter feeling.

Choose a time when it is not so crowded to go to the washroom. Place your towel over your left arm. The open ends of the folded towel may hang on either the inside or outside of your arm. When you leave your seat, stand up straight and walk lightly, taking the most convenient way to the back entrance. Gently lift the screen with both hands and exit the monks' hall. If your seat is in the higher section [north part of the hall], you should exit through the north side of the back entrance with your right foot first. If your seat is in the lower section [south part of the hall], you should exit through the south side of the back entrance with your left foot first. Do not make noise by dragging your sandals or stomping.

When you walk by the study hall or the well house and come across someone, do not exchange words. Even if you don't come across anyone, do not chant or sing to yourself. Hold your hands in isshu;* do not let your arms dangle, and do not allow your sleeves to fall over your hands. When you get to the washroom, wait until a sink is available; do not jostle with others for position. As soon as you find a place at the sink, wash your face.

To wash your face, first put your towel around your neck with one end on either side. Holding one end in each hand, bring them under the armpits toward the back, cross the two sides on the back, bring both ends under the armpits again, and tie them on the chest. This is the same as tying up the sleeves of your robe with a cloth belt. In this way the front edges of the robe and sleeves are tied up higher than the elbows and lower than the shoulders.

Then take up the willow twig and chant in gassho:

Holding this willow twig
I vow to unfold the true dharma
natural heart of purity
with all sentient beings.

Chew the willow twig to clean your teeth and then chant:

Chewing this willow twig in the morning
I vow to tame these fangs
and cut through desires
with all sentient beings.

The Buddha said, "Do not chew more than one-third of the willow twig." Follow the guidelines when you clean your teeth or scrape your tongue. Do not scrape your tongue more than three times. Stop scraping if you notice any bleeding.

There is an old saying: "For cleansing your mouth, chew your willow twig and rinse your mouth." If someone is facing you, cover your mouth with your hand to avoid disgusting him. Find a place where you are not observed when you spit or blow your nose. Although most monasteries in Song China have no designated place to use the willow twigs in their washrooms, our Daibutsu Monastery* does have a place for that.

Take a wooden basin with both hands and place it at the hearth. Put warm water into the basin with a dipper. Bring the basin back to the sink, dip your hands in it lightly, and wash your face thoroughly. Cleanse your eyes, nostrils, ears, and mouth following this procedure. Do not waste the warm water. When you rinse your mouth, spit the water outside of the basin. Washing your face, bend over the basin; if you stand up straight, you are liable to splatter water on your neighbor's basin. Pick up some water by cupping your hands and wash your face without leaving any dirt or grime. Then untie the towel with the right hand and dry your face. If there is a common towel, you may use it as well. Be careful not to make knocking sounds with the basin and dipper. Do not cough or gargle loudly and startle those around you. In regard to this, there is an ancient saying: "Washing your face at the fifth night period is essential for practice of the way. Do not disturb the assembly by making spitting sounds and noise with the basins."

The manner for returning to the monks' hall is similar to going out from it. Getting back to your position, cover your body with the bedding again and do zazen following the form. You can decide for yourself whether or not to use the bedding. You do not wear the kashaya yet.

When you put on your daywear, do so at your seat. When getting dressed, cover yourself with your clothes and discreetly untie your belts. Drop your nightwear off your shoulders from behind so they are covering your lap, like you would cover it with the bedding quilt. Tie the belts around your clothes and put them in order. Then fold the nightwear and place it behind your seat. This is similar to the way you take off your daywear and put on your nightwear.

Do not reveal your naked body while changing clothes on your seat. Do not stand on the seat while folding your clothes. Do not make light of the assembly by fiddling with your beads or making grunting sounds. Do not converse with your neighbors while on the seat. Do not sit or lie down out of alignment with those on either side. Do not crawl off and on the platform. Do not make rustling sounds by brushing up against the platform with your sleeves or the skirt of your robe.

At the fifth night period, the han in front of the head monk's quarters is struck three times. After the abbot and head monk are seated, monks in the assembly refrain from entering and leaving through the front door. Do not put away the bed mat and quilt before unfolding the stillness.* The stillness of sitting is unfolded

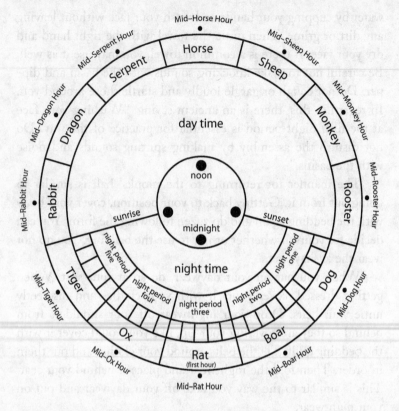

Time of the day. According to the traditional East Asian system, the daytime from sunrise to sunset is divided into six (five and two half) hours. The nighttime has six hours in the same manner. Hence the length of each hour changes daily. This diagram illustrates the case of a day in summer.

There are five night periods, each of which is divided into five segments. According to Dogen's instruction for the monastic practice, a night period is signaled by so many strikes of a drum, and a segment by so many strikes of a bell.

with the dovetailing sounds of the umpan* in front of the kitchen and the han in front of each of the halls. At this point you fold the sleeping mat and bedding quilt, put away the pillow, raise the curtain in front of your cabinet, and put the bedding away. Then put on your kashaya and sit facing each other. The screens on the windows and the front and back entrances are raised and incense and candles are lit in front of the figure of the Sacred Monk.

This is the way to fold the covering quilt: At the sounds for unfolding stillness, you take hold of two corners and fold it the long way, then fold it again the long way making four layers. Fold the ends in half twice making sixteen layers and place it behind the sleeping mat.

Then fold the sleeping mat and put it under the quilt. The pillow is inserted in between the folds of the quilt. When you place the quilt, the open edges are facing you. Bow with your palms together and place the kashaya wrapped in a cloth on top of the quilt with both hands. Bow again, open the wrapping cloth, and spread it over the bedding quilt. The cloth covers both sides of the folded quilt but not the ends. Then bow to the kashaya, lift it up with both hands, and put it on the top of your head. Then chant the verse "Vow of the Kashaya" while in gassho:

> Great is the robe of liberation,
> the robe of no form, the field of happiness.
> I wear the Tathagata's teaching
> to awaken countless beings.

After chanting, put on the kashaya, then turn to the right and sit facing out. When you fold the quilt, do not extend it beyond your own space. Do not be careless and noisy. Taking care of the body, mindful of the guidelines, respectfully go along with the assembly. Do not get out the bedding and go back to sleep after the unfolding of stillness. When the morning meal is over, go to the study hall, have tea or hot water, or go back to your place in the monk's hall and resume sitting.

Putting on kashaya.

After the morning meal just before midmorning zazen, the ino* hangs the plaque announcing zazen in front of the monks' hall. Then, the han is struck. The head monk and the assembly enter the hall with their kashaya on, are seated, and do zazen. While the head monk faces out, the officers* face the wall in the same way as the rest of the assembly. The abbot sits on his chair. During zazen, you are not supposed to look around and peer at the faces of those going in and out.

If you need to go to the toilet, first take off the kashaya and place it on the folded covering quilt [behind you] while you are still seated, bow in gassho, and get down from the platform. To get off the platform, face the front by turning to the right and put your legs down. Then put on your sandals and leave. While leaving and entering, do not stare at the back of the heads of those who are doing zazen.

Keep your eyes down while walking. Do not walk with your

feet ahead and your body leaning back, rather align your body and feet together. Keep your gaze on the floor about one hiro [ten shaku, about ten feet] ahead. Your step should be about the same as a half length of your foot. Slow and quiet walking is regarded as excellent. It should be just like standing, as if you were not taking a step. Do not make a disturbance by rudely dragging your sandals. Hold your hands in isshu covered with your sleeves; do not let your arms down.

Do not fold your kashaya while standing on the platform. Do not hold the corners of your kashaya with your mouth. Do not shake out your kashaya. Do not fold it by using your foot on it or by holding it under your chin. Do not hold the kashaya with wet hands. Do not hang it on the Sacred Monk's altar or let it drape over the edge of the platform. Do not sit on the edges of the kashaya. Always be aware of the kashaya and keep it in good order. Bow before putting it on. It is also a custom to bow after taking it off and folding it. You should not ignore this. During zazen, do not leave your seat and go out with your kashaya on.

Hearing the umpan from the kitchen, the monks bow together. This marks the end of zazen. Then they leave the monks' hall with their kashaya on. The cushions are left on the seats and are put away after the midday meal. After hearing the umpan, the ino has his attendant put away the zazen plaque. This plaque is put up during the midmorning zazen, and at no other time. At the beginning of the off-day, a plaque announcing it is hung. This is taken away after the evening bell.

The hans are struck for midmorning zazen, and the bell is struck for zazen at dusk. These are the times when the monks wear their kashaya and sit facing the wall. For afternoon and late evening zazen, they sit without wearing the kashaya. In the afternoon, the monks enter the hall wearing their work robes, put their cushions on their seats, and do zazen without spreading the sleeping mats. There is also a traditional way to half spread the sleeping mats on the platform. Taking off the day clothes, fold them and put them on the covering quilt before doing zazen. For late evening zazen, keep your kashaya on top of the cabinet.

For zazen, always use a zafu.* One way to sit is in a full-lotus position: Place the right foot on the left thigh and the left foot on the right thigh. Or you may sit in a half-lotus position by simply placing the left foot on the right thigh. Place the right hand palm up on the left foot and the left hand on the right palm, with the ends of the thumbs lightly touching each other. Then straighten your body and sit erect. The top of the head and backbone are aligned and support each other, without leaning to one side, bending forward or backward. The ears should be in alignment with the shoulders, and the nose with the navel. Rest your tongue against the roof of your mouth. The lips and teeth should be closed. The eyes should be open, neither too wide nor too narrow; do not allow the eyelids to close. Do not let your head and neck get out of line with your backbone.

Let the breath pass naturally through your nose. Neither panting nor being noisy, let the breath be neither too long nor too short.

To begin zazen adjust your body and mind and relax yourself inside and out by exhaling fully several times and swaying your body from side to side seven or eight times. Sit solidly in samadhi and think not thinking. How do you think not thinking? Beyond thinking. This is the essential art of zazen.

When you get up from zazen, do so slowly. When you get off the platform, do so slowly and mindfully. Do not walk with a big stride or move hastily. Keep your hands joined together inside your sleeves. Do not let your hands and sleeves hang down. Walk slowly with your eyes slightly down. Do not look around. Be careful not to walk hurriedly and inattentively. In accordance with each situation, take a humble and harmonious attitude and blend with the assembly. These are the standards for the endeavor of the way.

Walking meditation.

Guidelines for hosan*: [*The Guidelines for the Zen Monasteries* says,] "The hosan follows the afternoon zazen." After the midday meal the assembly of monks puts away their cushions, leaves the monks' hall, retires to the study hall, and sits on the reading platform. In the early afternoon, they return to the monks' hall, take out their cushions, and sit zazen. After zazen,

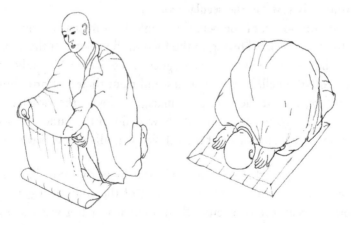

Spreading the bowing mat in three folds and making a full bow.

the cushions are left where they are until the midday meal the following day.

Before the hosan, the shuso,* starting from the walkway on the north side of the hall, enters from the south [left] side of the main [east] entrance. He may hit the han in front of his quarters three times before entering. He then offers incense to the Sacred Monk and takes his seat. He may also circumambulate the hall one time after offering incense, before taking his seat. Then, the doan* announces the seating of the shuso throughout the monastery by hitting the han in front of the study hall three times.

The monks enter the hall, put on their kashayas at their seats, and sit facing the aisle. Those who have been sitting facing the wall also put on their kashaya, turn around, and face the aisle. The doan first reports to the abbot and then hangs the hosan plaque. The doan lifts the screen in front of the hall. He enters the hall, bows to the Sacred Monk, goes to the shuso's seat, and bows to him with gassho. Then with his hands in shashu, he leans forward and whispers to the shuso, "Reverend—Hôsan." The doan goes back to the Sacred Monk, bows, stands up straight with his hands in shashu, and announces in a strong drawn-out voice, "Hô-ô-ô-san." He proceeds out of the hall and hits the hosan bell three times. (This corresponds to the mid-rooster hour [around six P.M.] in the secular world.)

At the sound of the bell, the monks bow in shashu and bow in the same way as bowing to the food in their bowl. If the abbot is in the hall, he stands up, bows, goes to the Sacred Monk, bows, and exits the hall. The monks descend from their platform, bow as before, spread their sleeping mats, and lower the closet curtains. They go to the study hall, bow again in the same manner, and sit facing each other at their desks. It is all right to have tea.

In the event that tea is offered formally in the study hall, the monk whose turn it is to be the head of the study hall gets up from his seat, offers incense, then offers tea or hot water at the altar.

The monk may wear his ordinary day clothes or put on his kashaya, according to the direction of the abbot or the custom of the monastery. The way he offers incense is as follows: He faces the main image, makes a standing bow with palms together, and walks up to the incense burner in front of the altar. He offers incense with his right hand, then holding his hands in shashu, turns around to the right facing away from the altar and returns to his original position facing the altar. He makes a standing bow and walks holding his hands in shashu and stops between the two platforms of the northern section of the study hall. He makes a standing bow to those who are seated there. He turns all the way around to the right, walks past the center, stops between the two platforms of the southern section of the study hall, and makes a standing bow. Again, he turns to the right, walks to the front of the altar, makes a standing bow to the main image, and stands in shashu.

Then, tea or hot water is served. After that, incense is offered as before.

PRACTICE PERIOD*

IN AN INFORMAL TALK to open the summer practice period, Rujing, my late master Tiantong, Old Buddha, presented this poem:

> Piling up bones in an open field,
> gouging out a cave in empty sky,
> break through the barrier of dualism
> and splash in a bucket of pitch-black lacquer.

To grab hold of this spirit, to train constantly for thirty years, eating meals, sleeping, and stretching your legs, this requires unstinting support. The structure of the ninety-day summer practice period provides such support. It is the head and face of buddhas and ancestors. It has been intimately transmitted as their skin, flesh, bones, and marrow. You turn the buddha ancestors' eyes and heads into the days and months of the ninety-day summer practice period. Regard the whole of each practice period as the entity of buddhas and ancestors.

From top to bottom the summer practice period is buddha ancestors. It covers everything without an inch of land or a speck of earth left out. The summer practice period is an anchoring peg that is neither new nor old, that has never arrived and will never leave. It's the size of your fist and takes the form of grabbing you by the nose. When the practice period is opened, the empty sky cracks apart and all of space is dissolved. When the practice period is closed, the earth explodes, leaving no place undisturbed.

When the koan of opening the summer practice period is taken up, it looks as if something has arrived. When the fishing nets and birds' nests of the summer practice period are all thrown away, it looks as if something has left. However, those who participated intimately in the practice period have been covered with opening and closing all along. An inch of grass has not appeared for ten thousand miles, so you might say, "Give me back the meal money for these ninety days."

Priest Sixin* of Mt. Huanglong said, "My pilgrimage of more than thirty years amounts to one ninety-day summer practice period, not a day more, not a day less."

Thus, after a pilgrimage of more than thirty years, you develop an eye that sees summer itself as a ninety-day practice period. Even if you try to stretch it or contract it, the ninety days will always bounce back and be just ninety days. You yourself cannot leap over the boundary of ninety days, but if you use the ninety days as your hands and feet, you can make the leap. Although the ninety-day summer practice period serves as a support for us, the buddha ancestors did not create it on our behalf. They only handed it down to us from the past, heir to heir, authentically.

Thus, to experience a summer practice period is to experience all buddhas and all ancestors. To experience a summer practice period is to see buddhas and ancestors directly. Buddhas and ancestors have been produced by the summer practice period for a long, long time. Although the ninety-day summer practice period is only as long as your forehead, it is beyond time. One kalpa,* ten kalpas, one hundred, one thousand, or innumerable kalpas cannot contain it. Although ordinary events can be contained within one thousand or innumerable kalpas, the ninety days contain one hundred, one thousand, or innumerable kalpas. Even if the innumerable kalpas experience the ninety days and see the buddhas, the ninety days are still free of innumerable kalpas. Thus, investigate that the ninety-day summer practice period is as long as an eyeball. The body and mind of the practice period is just like that.

To become fully immersed in the liveliness of the summer practice period is to be free of the liveliness of the summer practice period. Although it has origination and cause, it has not come from another place or another time, nor has it arisen here and now. When you grasp for the origination of the ninety-day period, it immediately appears. When you search for the cause of the ninety-day period, it's immediately right here. Although ordinary people and sages use the ninety-day period as their abode and sustenance, it is beyond the boundary of ordinary and sacred. It is also beyond the reach of discernment and nondiscernment, and even beyond beyond the reach of discernment and nondiscernment.

During a dharma talk that the World-honored One gave in the country of Magadha,* he announced his intention to go into a summer retreat. He said to Ananda,* "My advanced disciples, the four types of human and celestial practitioners* are not truly paying attention to my dharma talk, so I have decided to enter Indra's* cave and spend the ninety days of summer in sitting practice. If people should come to ask about the dharma, please give them your explanation on my behalf. Nothing arises and nothing perishes." Then, he closed the entrance to his meditation chamber and sat. It has been 2,194 years since then.[1] Today is the third year of the Kangen Era [1245].

Those who haven't entered the inner chamber regard the World-honored One's retreat in the country of Magadha as proof of expounding the dharma without words. These confused people think, "The Buddha's closing off his chamber and spending the summer in solitary sitting shows that words and speech are merely skillful means* and cannot indicate the truth. Cutting off words

1. Recent scholarship indicates that Shakyamuni lived in the fifth century BCE, about 1,600–1,700 years before Dogen's time.

and eliminating mental activity is therefore the ultimate truth. Wordlessness and mindlessness is real; words and thoughts are unreal. The Buddha sat in the closed chamber for ninety days in order to cut off all human traces."

Those who say such things are greatly mistaken about the World-honored One's true intention. If you really understand the meaning of cutting off words, speech, and mental activity, you will see that all social and economic endeavors are essentially already beyond words, speech, and mental activity. Going beyond words and speech is itself all words and speech, and going beyond mental activity is nothing but all mental activity. So, it is a misunderstanding of this story to see it as advocating the overthrow of words, speech, and mental activity. Reality is to go into the mud and enter the weeds* and expound the dharma for the benefit of others; turning the dharma and saving all beings is not something optional. If people who call themselves descendants of the Buddha insist on thinking that the Buddha's ninety days of solitary summer sitting mean that words, speech, and mental activity are transcended, they should demand a refund of those ninety days of summer sitting.

Also, do not misunderstand the Buddha's further words to Ananda, *Please give them your explanation on my behalf. Nothing arises and nothing perishes.* Because the Buddha's closing the room and sitting through the summer is not merely an activity without words and speech, ask the World-honored One, in Ananda's place, "What is the meaning of 'nothing arises and nothing perishes,' and how do you practice it?" In the light of your question, examine the World-honored One's teaching.

This story about the Buddha contains the primary truth and the primary beyond-truth of his expounding and turning the dharma. It is a mistake to use it as proof that the Buddha taught abandonment of words and speech. If you see it that way, it is like taking a three-foot dragon-fountain sword and hanging it up on the wall of a potter's shop to be used as a shaping knife.

Thus, sitting for ninety days of summer is an ancient method used by authentic buddha ancestors for turning the dharma wheel. The important part of this story is just the Buddha announcing his intention to go into a summer retreat. This makes it quite clear that sitting the ninety-day summer practice period is something to be done without fail. Not to practice in this way is to be outside the way.

When the World-honored One was alive, he held the summer practice period in Tushita Heaven or he held it, with five hundred monks, in a hall on Vulture Peak. It didn't matter to him what part of India he was in; he always held a summer practice period when the time came. Buddha ancestors for generations up to the present have been practicing it as the essential matter; it is the unsurpassable way of practice and enlightenment. In the *Indra's Net Sutra,** the winter practice period is mentioned, but that tradition has not been passed on; only the ninety-day summer practice period has come down to us, correctly transmitted for fifty-one generations up to the present.

In *The Guidelines for Zen Monasteries,* it is written: "When a seeker comes to a monastery wanting to join in a practice period, he should arrive half a month in advance so that the welcoming tea and other entering rituals can be performed without haste."

Half a month in advance means the last part of the third month. Thus, one should arrive some time in the third month. The season for traveling to enroll in a monastery ends before the first day of the fourth month. After that, the guest office and the visitors' room close. By then, according to tradition, all monks wishing to reside in a monastery should have their traveling bags hanging either in the monks' quarters, or in the nearby quarters for laypeople. This is the style of the buddha ancestors, and it should be respected and practiced. By then the fists and nostrils [teachers and elders] should also have their bags in place.

However, a group of demons say that what is essential is the development of the Mahayana view, and that the summer practice period is a Hinayana* training and should not be followed.

Those who say such things have never seen or heard the buddha-dharma. A ninety-day summer practice period of sitting is itself complete perfect enlightenment. Both Mahayana and Hinayana have fine teachings and practices; these are all branches, leaves, flowers, and fruits of the ninety-day practice period.

On the third day of the fourth month, the official preparation begins. Preceding this, from the first day of the fourth month, the ino prepares a preliminary list of the names of the participants according to their dharma ordination seniority. On the third day of the fourth month, after the morning meal, the preliminary list is posted on the lattice window to the right of the entrance to the study hall. The list is posted every day after the morning meal and taken down after the bell that signals the end of the practice for the day. It is displayed this way from the third day until the fifth day of the fourth month.

Care must be taken with the order in which the names are arranged on the preliminary list. They are not listed according to the monastic offices held but according to seniority in ordination date. However, the titles of those who have served as officers in other monasteries should be written on the list, especially if they have served as head monk or administrator. If they have served in several positions, the title pertaining to the highest position they reached should appear on the list. Those who have been abbots should have the title "former abbot" added to their names. Sometimes, people who have served as abbots in small temples unknown to most monks prefer out of modesty not to be acknowledged as former abbots. Also, there are monks who have served as senior teachers in monks' halls, and as such have sat in the "former abbot" seat in the hall, without however actually having served as abbots. The listing of such monks should not include the title "former abbot." In such cases the title "senior monk" can be used. If they volunteer to serve as humble caretakers of the abbot's robes and bowls or his incense attendants, as they often do, this can be an excellent example. Other senior monks will be appointed to various positions by the teacher. Some monks who have previously trained in small monasteries, including those who have been abbots of small temples, might be invited to serve as head monk, secretary,* treasurer, or administrator in large monasteries. Because it is not unusual for people to make fun of positions in minor monasteries or temples, such monks may prefer not to acknowledge their past positions.

The following is an example of such a list:

> In the such-and-such monastery on such-and-such mountain in such-and-such province of such-and-such country, the names in the ocean assembly forming the summer practice period are as follows:
>
> Venerable Ajnatakaundinya* [the first disciple of the Buddha], Chief monk
> Priest ——, Abbot
> Ordained in the first year of the Kempo Era
> ——, Senior monk
> ——, Sutra storehouse keeper
> ——, Senior monk
> ——, Senior monk
> Ordained in the second year of the Kempo Era
> ——, Former abbot
> ——, Ino
> ——, Head monk
> ——, Guest manager*
> ——, Senior monk
> ——, Bathhouse keeper
> Ordained in the first year of the Kenreki Era
> ——, Work leader*
> ——, Attendant monk
> ——, Head monk
> ——, Head monk
> ——, Lay contact monk
> ——, Senior monk

————, Tenzo*
————, Infirmary manager
Ordained in the third year of the Kenreki Era
————, Secretary
————, Senior monk
————, Former abbot
————, Head monk
————, Senior monk
————, Senior monk

I respectfully present this preliminary list. Please notify me if there is a mistake.
Sincerely yours, monk [so-and-so], Ino
The third day, the fourth month, the year ————

This is calligraphed in formal script on a white sheet of paper. Cursive or decorative script is not used. This list is fastened to a paperboard with a flax string; it is about the thickness of two grains of rice; and it hangs like a screen. It is removed at the end of zazen on the fifth day of the fourth month.

On the eighth day of the fourth month, the Buddha's Birthday* is celebrated.

On the thirteenth day, after the midday meal, the study hall monks are served tea and treats and do melodic sutra chanting in the study hall. The study hall director is in charge of this event, and it is he who boils the water and offers the incense. He takes his position at the end of the hall in the middle [the place of highest honor], while the study hall head monk is positioned to the left of the enshrined image. However, it is the study hall director who rises to offer incense. The head monk and officers of the monastery do not join in this sutra chanting. Only the study hall monks participate in this ceremony.

The ino hangs the revised list of participants on the east wall in front of the monks' hall after the morning meal on the fifteenth. It hangs near where the monastery officers sit for meditation practice on the south side. *The Guidelines for Zen Monasteries* says, "The ino prepares the list of participants beforehand and offers incense and flowers. He hangs the list in front of the monks' hall."

On the fourteenth day of the fourth month, after the midday meal, a sign announcing the chanting ceremony is hung in front of the monks' hall as well as other halls. By the evening, officers have set up incense and flowers in front of the sign outside the shrine of the local earth deities, and the monks assemble.

This is the procedure for the ceremony: After the monks assemble, the abbot offers incense, then the officers and the heads of departments offer incense in a way similar to the style of offering made during the ceremony of bathing the Buddha [on Buddha's Birthday]. Then, the ino comes forward, makes a standing bow to the abbot, bows to the local earth deities, faces north, and chants as follows:

> As we reflect quietly, fragrant winds waft over the fields, and the god of summer holds dominion in all directions. At this time the Dharma King* ordains that the monks remain secluded in the monastery, and on this day the children of Shakyamuni invoke the life-protecting deities. We assembled here, honor the shrine of spirits, and chant the great names of myriad virtues, dedicating offerings to the deities enshrined here. We earnestly request for protection and complete accomplishment of the practice period. Now, we invoke the venerable ones (after each of the following names a small bell is struck): Pure Dharmakaya* Vairochana Buddha, Complete Sambhogakaya* Lochana Buddha, Uncountable Nirmanakaya* Shakyamuni Buddha, Future Maitreya Buddha, All Buddhas throughout space and time, Great Sacred Manjushri* Bodhisattva, Great Sacred Samantabhadra* Bodhisattva, Great Compassion Avalokiteshvara Bodhisattva, All Venerable Bodhisattva-Mahasattvas,* Maha

Prajna Paramita.* We dedicate the merit of our chanting and offerings to the dragon deities of the earth who protect the true dharma. May the wisdom light illuminate and activate this merit so that pure enjoyment and selfless happiness will arise. We again invoke All Buddhas throughout space and time, All Venerable Bodhisattva-Mahasattvas, and the Maha Prajna Paramita.

A drum is hit and the monks go for ceremonial tea in the monks' hall. Serving the tea is the responsibility of the monastery administrator.* The monks enter the hall with a formal circumambulation and sit in their positions facing the center of the hall; the officer in charge opens the ceremony with an incense offering. *The Guidelines for Zen Monasteries* says, "This ceremony is usually conducted by the monastery administrator, but the ino may substitute for him."

Prior to the chanting ceremony the officer in charge calligraphs an announcement of invitation to the tea ceremony and presents it to the head monk in the following manner: The officer wears the kashaya and carries the formal bowing cloth.* He faces the head monk, makes three semiformal bows* or makes greeting bows by spreading the bowing cloth twice,* and presents the announcement to the head monk who responds by bowing in the same way. The announcement is presented in a box in which a fine silk cloth has been placed; the box is carried ceremonially by an assistant. The officer bringing the announcement is escorted into and later out of the hall by the head monk. The announcement reads:

> This evening I will serve tea in the monks' hall for the head monk and everyone in the assembly to establish the practice period. Please kindly attend.
> Respectfully yours,
> Monk so-and-so, Monastery Administrator
> The fourteenth day of the fourth month, the third day of the Kangen Era

This is signed with the first character of the administrator's name. After presenting the announcement to the head monk, the administrator has his assistant post it in front of the monks' hall. There is a varnished bulletin board to the south of the front entrance, to which envelopes for announcements are fastened with bamboo pegs. The envelope for tea invitations is posted next to them. There is a traditional format for writing such an invitation. The size of characters should not exceed five *bu* [approximately half an inch]. On the front of the envelope, write: "Attention: the Head Monk and the Assembly. From Monastery Administrator." This announcement is removed after tea is served.

Before the morning meal of the fifteenth day of the fourth month, the monastery officers, heads of work crews, teachers, and dharma associates assemble at the abbot's quarters to greet the abbot. However, he may exempt the monks from this procedure by placing, on the previous day, a poetic statement of dharma words on the eastern side of the entrance to his room or in front of the monks' hall.

After the dharma talk is delivered from the high seat in the dharma hall,* the abbot descends the steps, stands on the northern end of the bowing mat* placed in the center, and faces south. The monastery officers approach him and make ceremonial greeting by spreading the bowing cloths twice in the following manner: First, they spread their bowing cloths and make three formal bows, and then say, "In this practice period of seclusion, we have the opportunity to serve you intimately. With the beneficence of your dharma guidance, we are confident that no disturbance will occur." Then, they spread their bowing cloths again and make three formal bows again. They fold up their bowing cloths and place them on their arms under their sleeves, approach closer to the abbot, and make a seasonal greeting by saying, "Now, it is the beginning of the summer and the days are gradually getting warmer. This is the time of year when the Dharma King first established a practice period. We are all grateful that you now enjoy good health of mind and body. This is very auspicious."

Then, they make three semiformal bows and remain silent. The abbot returns each of the officers' bows.

The abbot replies, "We are extremely fortunate to be able to have this practice period together. I hope that Head Monk so-and-so and Monastery Administrator so-and-so and other leaders will support one another so as to prevent any disturbance from arising."

The head monk and the assembly of monks then come forward and repeat the same process of greeting with the abbot. At this time, the head monk, officers, and other monks all face north and bow. The abbot alone faces south and stands in front of the dharma seat steps. His bowing cloth is spread on the main bowing mat.

Then, the head monk and the entire assembly spread their bowing cloths twice, making three greeting bows to the abbot. As they do this, those who are not fully participating in the practice period, including the junior monks, the attendant monks, the senior dharma family members, as well as the novices, stand to the side along the east wall of the dharma hall. However, if there are strips of paper with donors' names on the east wall, they should stand near the big drum in the northeast corner or along the west wall.

After these bows the officers go to the kitchen and stand in the ceremonial location. The head monk leads the assembly there and greets the officers with three semiformal bows. During this time, the junior monks, the attendant monks, and the senior dharma family members all pay their respects to the abbot in the dharma hall in the following manner: Senior dharma family members spread their bowing cloths twice and make greeting bows. The abbot returns their bows. The junior monks and attendant monks make nine formal bows. The abbot does not return their bows. Novices may make nine or twelve bows. The abbot responds to these bows by putting his palms together.

After the ceremony in the kitchen, the head monk and the assembly proceed to the monks' hall. The head monk stands outside near the entrance, on the north side, facing south toward the monks who are gathered outside. The monks make three semiformal bows to the head monk. Then, the head monk enters the monks' hall followed by the assembly in the order of ordination seniority, and they circumambulate the hall. Then, each monk stands in his respective position. The officers enter the hall, spread their bowing cloths fully open, and make three [most formal] bows to the enshrined image. They make three semiformal bows in front of the head monk, and the assembly returns their bows. The officers circumambulate the hall once, go to their positions, and stand with their hands folded.

Then, the abbot enters the hall, offers incense to the enshrined image, fully spreads his bowing cloth, and makes three bows and stands. As he does this, the junior monks [who have entered the hall after the assembly] are standing behind the enshrined image, while the senior dharma family members are standing behind the assembly. The abbot goes to his seat, stands facing west, and makes three semiformal bows that are returned by the head monk and the assembly.

The abbot circumambulates the hall and exits. The head monk stands at the south side of the doorway of the hall in order to bow to the abbot as he leaves. Then, the head monk and the assembly face each other, spread the bowing cloth folded in three, make three formal bows, and say, "We now have the good fortune to participate in this practice period. May unwholesome karma of body, speech, and mind not arise and may we practice with compassion for one another." The head monk, secretary, head of the storehouse, and other officers go back to their offices. The monks who live in the monks' residence hall make three semiformal bows to the hall director and the head monk of the hall, and make the same statement that was made in the monks' hall.

The abbot then makes the rounds of the monastery buildings starting with the kitchen and ending with the abbot's quarters. This procedure is conducted as follows:

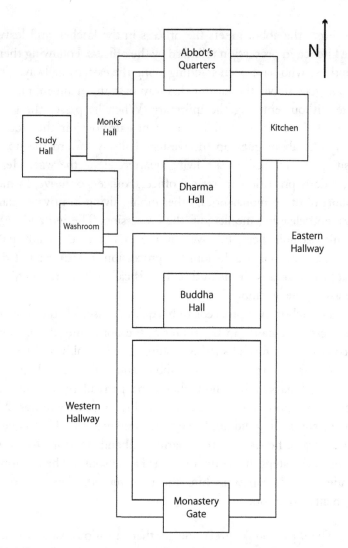

N

Abbot's Quarters

Monks' Hall

Study Hall

Kitchen

Dharma Hall

Washroom

Eastern Hallway

Buddha Hall

Western Hallway

Monastery Gate

Eihei-ji: presumed original layout. The ground plan of the Eihei Monastery at Dogen's time no longer exists. The original buildings were burned in 1473. The presumed layout presented here is based on the 1752 map of the reconstructed buildings. It has been modified in accordance with Dogen's accounts in "Practice Period," which imply the approximate location of other buildings: East side, south of the kitchen: infirmary. West side, south of the monks hall (from north): the offices of the ino and the head monk, monks' private living quarters.

First, the abbot greets the officers in the kitchen and leaves the kitchen in procession followed by the officers. Following them are those who have been standing along the eastern hallway. The abbot goes down the eastern hallway past the main monastery gate without entering the infirmary. When he passes the gate, those stationed in the buildings near the gate now join the procession. The abbot goes up the western hallway toward the north visiting the monks' private living quarters along the way. Here, the elderly practitioners, retired officers, officers on leave, former abbots of other monasteries, other monks living in private quarters, and cleaning monks join the procession. The ino and head monk also join here, followed by the monks in the study hall. Thus, the various monks join the procession in turn each at the place associated with his duties. This is called "the procession of amassing the assembly."

The abbot then proceeds to his quarters, ascends the stairs to the west, and stands in the center of the north end of the room facing south in formal shashu posture. The assembly and the officers all face north, toward the abbot, and make a standing bow to him. This standing bow should be particularly formal and deep. The abbot returns their bow, and the assembly retires. My late master Rujing did not bring the assembly to the abbot's quarters; instead, he went to the dharma hall and stood in shashu in front of the steps of the dharma seat facing south. The assembly made a standing bow to him and then retired. This is also an authentic tradition.

Then, the monks greet one another in various ways, according to their relationships. "Greet" here means that they bow to one another. For example, groups from the same home region greet one another with a feeling of celebration, appreciating the opportunity of sharing the same practice period together. Many people make these greetings in the Hall of Light* [study hall]; others greet one another along the hallways. The monks may use the greeting phrases used in the monks' hall ceremony, or they may say something spontaneous. When disciples meet their root teachers,* they greet them with nine formal bows. The dharma family members of the abbot greet him by spreading the bowing cloths twice and making three greeting bows or by spreading the bowing cloth fully and making three formal bows. Monks accompanying the dharma family members make their greeting in the same way. Among others who should be greeted formally are dharma uncles, those who sit nearby on the meditation platform, and those who have practiced together in the past. Those monks who live in the private quarters, the head monk, the secretary, the storehouse keeper, the guest manager, and the bath master as well as the treasurer, monastery administrator, ino, tenzo, work leader, former abbots of other monasteries, senior nuns, and lay practitioners should visit one another's quarters and offer greeting bows.

If the entrances to the common quarters become crowded with monks, so that it is difficult to enter, a note is left attached to the doorway. The note, on a small piece of white paper about one *sun* [about one inch] wide and two *suns* tall, should read, "Monk Soun (for example) of such and such quarters offers greeting," or the note may be from several monks, "Monks Soun, Esho (and others if there are any) offer greetings." Other options for the note are "Salutations from Monk so-and-so," "Respectful greetings from Monk so-and-so," "With greetings from Monk so-and-so," or "With bows from Monk so-and-so." These are several examples, but there are many other ways this card can be written. It is not unusual for there to be many cards attached to the doorways, always on the right-hand side, never on the left [considered the higher side] to be respectful. The director of each of the quarters removes the cards after the midday meal. On this day all the living quarters large and small have their entrance screens* rolled up.

Traditionally, at this point the abbot, monastery administrator, and the head monk in turn serve tea; however, in remote monasteries on distant islands or in the deep mountains, this custom may be omitted. Retired elders and senior monks with teaching status serve tea for officers and heads of crews in their own quarters.

After opening the practice period with this thorough ceremony, monks now make endeavors in the way. Those who have not participated in a summer practice period, regardless of other ways they may have practiced, are not descendents of buddha ancestors, nor can they themselves be buddha ancestors. The practice of the Jeta Grove and Vulture Peak are all actualized by the way of practice period. Practice period is the field of enlightenment, the mind seal of buddha ancestors, where buddha ancestors dwell.

The summer practice period draws to a close with the following events: On the thirteenth day of the seventh month, sutras are chanted in the study hall, followed by formal serving of tea and refreshments. The monk who is serving as head of the study hall for that month officiates at these ceremonies.

On the fourteenth day of the seventh month, there is a chanting ceremony in the evening.

On the fifteenth day of that month, the abbot ascends the dharma seat to give a formal talk. The procedure of individual greetings, formal visits to the living quarters, and tea ceremony are similar to those at the opening of practice period. However, the words for the announcement of the tea ceremony should be written as follows:

> The administrator will serve refreshments in the monks' hall this evening to honor the head monk and the assembly in celebration of our completion of the practice period. He requests the attendance of all.
> Signed respectfully,
> Monk so-and-so, Administrator.

Also the chant at the shrine for the earth-guarding deities is presented as follows:

The golden wind blows over the fields and the White Emperor governs the four quarters. Now, it is time to release the practice period of the King of Enlightenment; on this day the dharma year is complete. The ninety days have passed without obstruction and the assembly is at ease. We chant the broad names of all buddhas and make offerings to the enshrined spirits. The assembly of monks chants these words with deep respect.

The invocation of buddhas' names that follows is the same as at the beginning of practice period.

After the abbot's talk is over, the officers say in gratitude, "We respectfully rejoice that the dharma year has been completed without obstruction. This is due to the guidance of the master. We are extremely grateful."

The abbot responds by saying, "Now, the dharma year is complete. I would like to express my gratitude to Head Monk so-and-so, to Monastery Administrator so-and-so, and to all others whose dharma efforts mutually supported the practice period. I am extremely grateful."

The head monk and the assembly of the monks' hall, the head of the dormitory, and others all say in gratitude, "During the ninety-day summer period, unwholesome acts of body, speech, and mind may have disturbed the assembly. If so, we beg forgiveness and ask for your compassion."

The officers and heads of crews say, "Brothers in the assembly, if any of you are going traveling, please do so at your convenience after the concluding tea." (Some may leave earlier if it is necessary).

Since the time of the King of the Empty Eon, there has been no practice higher than this practice. Buddha ancestors have valued it exclusively, and it is the only thing that has remained free of the confusion caused by demons and deluded people outside the way. In India, China, and Japan, all descendents of buddha ancestors have participated in the practice period, but deluded people outside the way have never engaged in it. Because it is the original heart of the single great matter of buddha ancestors, this teaching of practice period is the content of what is expounded from the morning of the Buddha's attaining the way until the evening of pari-nirvana. There are Five Schools of home-leavers in India, but they equally maintain a ninety-day summer practice period and without fail practice it and realize the way; and in China none of the monks in the Nine Schools* have ever ignored the summer practice period. Those who have never participated in the summer practice period in their lifetimes cannot be called buddha disciples or monks. Practice period is not only a causal factor; it is itself practice-realization, it is itself the fruit of practice. The World-honored One, the Great Enlightened One, practiced and realized without missing one summer practice period in his whole lifetime. Know that summer practice period is buddha realization within the fruit of enlightenment.

This being so, those who call themselves descendents of buddha ancestors without engaging in the practice realization of a ninety-day summer practice period should be ridiculed. In fact ridicule would be more than they deserve! Simply pay no attention whatsoever to them: do not speak with them, do not sit with them, and do not walk in the same paths with them. In buddha-dharma the ancient way to cure those with such mistaken views is simply to shut them out with silence.

Understand and maintain a ninety-day summer practice as the buddha ancestors themselves. The correct transmission of the practice period tradition was handed down from the Seven Original Buddhas to Mahakashyapa, and through him it was correctly transmitted heir to heir to the Twenty-Eighth Indian Ancestor [Bodhidharma]. He in turn went to China and correctly transmitted it to the Second Ancestor, Huike, Great Master Pujue. From Huike it has been correctly transmitted heir to heir down to the present day. Thus, the tradition of practice period entered

China and was correctly transmitted in the assemblies of buddha ancestors, and accordingly it was correctly transmitted to Japan.

By sitting zazen in the ninety-day summer practice period within this assembly of correct transmission, you correctly receive the dharma of summer. Living with a true teacher and fully participating in the practice period makes the practice period a true practice period. Because the tradition of practice period has been transmitted face to face, heir to heir directly from practice periods practiced during the Buddha's own lifetime, it must be the correct and personal transmission of buddha face, of ancestor face, the complete merging with the realization of buddha ancestors' body and mind intimately and immediately.

Therefore, to see a practice period is to see buddha, to realize a practice period is to realize buddha, to practice a practice period is to practice buddha, to hear a practice period is to hear buddha, to study a practice period is to study buddha. Now, a ninety-day practice period is the inviolable dharma of all buddha ancestors. Therefore, even kings of the human world, Indra world, or Brahma world should make an effort to participate in a practice period as monks even for one summer, for to do so is to actually see buddha. Humans, devas, or dragons should participate in the ninety-day practice period as monks or nuns even if it is only once in a lifetime, for to practice this practice period is to actually see buddha, and all those who have joined the assembly of buddha ancestors to practice a ninety-day practice period have seen buddhas.

If we are fortunate enough to practice a summer practice period before our dewlike life drops down, whether in the realm of humans or devas, we will surely replace our skin, flesh, bones, and marrow with the skin, flesh, bones, and marrow of buddha ancestors. During every practice period, it is the buddha ancestors who come to practice the practice with everyone, and everyone who participates in the practice period practices as a buddha ancestor. Because of this those who engage in a practice period are called "one thousand buddhas and ten thousand ancestors." The reason for this is that a practice period is the skin, flesh, bones, and marrow as well as mind, consciousness, and body of buddha ancestors. Practice period is the top of the head, the eye, the fists, nostrils, the buddha nature circle drawn in the air, the whisk, wooden staff, bamboo stick, and sitting mat of buddha ancestors. Practice period is neither creating something new nor reusing something old.

The World-honored One said to Complete Enlightenment Bodhisattva* and all those in the assembly, as well as to all beings:

> Those who participate in the three-month summer practice period should abide as pure bodhisattvas, their minds free from the world's chattering, uninvolved with the world's opinions.
>
> On the opening day of the practice period make a statement like this in front of the buddha image: 'I—monk, nun, layman or laywoman so-and-so—now mount the bodhisattva vehicle in order to activate the practice of tranquility and together with all beings enter the true mark of purity and abide in it so that we can all make complete enlightenment our temple. The wisdom of equanimity and the freedom of nirvana are without boundaries; I pay homage to them. Without being influenced by the opinions of the world, I will engage in the three-month practice period with all the tathagatas and great bodhisattvas of the ten directions. Because I am now embarking on the practice of the great cause of the unsurpassable wondrous enlightenment of all the bodhisattvas, I am free of the bondage of the world.
>
> Good bodhisattva, this is a practice period that manifests bodhisattvas.

Thus, when monks, nuns, laymen, or laywomen participate in a three-month practice period, they invariably practice the great cause of unsurpassable wondrous enlightenment together with tathagatas and great bodhisattvas in the ten directions. Note that it is not only monks and nuns who participate in the practice period, laymen and laywomen also participate.

The place of this practice period is great complete enlightenment. Therefore, Vulture Peak and Jeta Grove are equally tathagatas' temples of great complete enlightenment. You should hear and understand the World-honored One's teaching that tathagatas and great bodhisattvas of the ten directions practice together in the three-month practice period.

The World-honored One held a ninety-day practice period in a monastery. On the last day, the day when all the monks are to confess their faults and ask for forgiveness, Manjushri suddenly appeared in the assembly.

Mahakashyapa asked Manjushri, "Where have you spent the summer practice period?"

Manjushri replied, "In three places [a demon's palace, a wealthy man's house, a house of prostitution]."

Mahakashyapa immediately assembled the monks to announce that Manjushri would be expelled; he lifted the mallet and was about to strike the bell, when he suddenly saw countless monasteries appear and in each of them there were a Manjushri and a Mahakashyapa. Just at the moment Mahakashyapa raised the mallet and was about to strike the sounding block signaling the expulsions of the multiple Manjushris that were in the multiple monasteries, the World-honored One said to Mahakashyapa, "Which of these Manjushris are you going to expel?"

Mahakashyapa was dumbfounded.

Keqin, Zen Master Yuanwu, commented on this: "An unstruck bell won't ring; an unbeaten drum won't sound. Mahakashyapa made it to the ferry station; Manjushri's sitting rides the waves through unlimited space. This is an excellent enactment of the buddha scene, but unfortunately Mahakashyapa missed one move. He should have responded to Old Man Shakyamuni's question by striking the bell; then he would have seen how the old boy destroys the whole world at once."

Keqin added a verse to this:

A great elephant doesn't play in a rabbit hutch.
Swallows and sparrows don't have the heart of an eagle.
Careful precision yet flowing with the wind,
hitting the mark and biting off the arrowhead.
The entire world is Manjushri.
The entire world is Mahakashyapa.
Solemnly they face each other—
who can be punished by Mahakashyapa?
One good swing—the Golden Ascetic [Mahakashyapa]
    drops it.

Thus, although the World-honored One practiced a practice period in one place while Manjushri practiced in three places, Manjushri was not a nonparticipant in the practice period. Those who are nonparticipants in the practice period are nonbuddhas and nonbodhisattvas. There are no descendents of buddha ancestors who are nonparticipants in practice period; all practice period participants are always descendents of buddha ancestors. Participation in the practice period is the body and mind, eye, and life energy of buddha ancestors. Those who do not abide peacefully in practice period are neither buddha ancestors nor descendents of buddha ancestors. Buddhas and bodhisattvas made of mud, wood, metal, or the seven precious substances all sit the three-month summer practice period together. Practice period is the buddha's instruction, an authentic custom that maintains the buddha-dharma-sangha Treasure. Those within the house of buddha ancestors should therefore wholeheartedly sit the three-month summer practice period.

Presented to the assembly of the Daibutsu Monastery, Echizen Province, on the thirteenth day, the sixth month, during the summer practice period, in the third year of the Kangen Era [1245].

Zazen through the Seasons

FORMAL TALKS

Recorded by Senne,* Ejo, and Gien,* Attendant Monks

Translators' introductory comments:

Each dharma year starts on the first day of the ninth lunar month. We present some of Dogen's words that mark major dharma events of the year. The three-month practice period, from the mid-fourth to the mid-seventh month, concludes the dharma year, and this is when a participant gains a dharma age. In Dogen's monastery, because of the intense summer climate in the midst of the practice period, formal zazen stops in the sixth month and resumes in the ninth month. In the following text, explanations by the translators are given in the headings.

[The dharma year begins with the striking of the han; formal zazen is resumed on the first day of the ninth month, after a three-month break at the hottest time of the year.]

This morning marks the first day of the ninth month, when we take out our cushions for zazen. But the event does not happen in this particular moment. It does not happen in the future, for example, before the feast on the fifth day of the month.

Steadfast thinking encircles the earth, vast karmic consciousness fills the sky. Even so, is it necessary to grasp the key to the gate of going beyond? (After a pause Dogen continued:) Just be present three thousand times in the morning and eight hundred times in the evening. At the right moment, be extremely careful not to miss the transmission of the stream.

[The monks' hall furnace is traditionally lit on the first day of the tenth month.]

Today the furnace opens its mouth
and widely proclaims stories from the sutras.
Kneading cold ash and the iron person
our minds glow red in front of our eyes.

[Winter solstice, the eleventh month]

Heaven has a singular clarity. Earth has renewed peacefulness. Each person attains ease. The season moves into light. This is the time when days become longer.

This is the timeless moment to attain buddha ancestors' infinite life. All of you aspire and practice within this timelessness. Endeavoring to follow the way, you must actualize one phrase. When timelessness is realized, you are powerful. When timelessness is realized, you are alive.

Bring forth the 360 days with beads made of buddha ancestors' body. What do you achieve day by day? Buddha ancestors' body and mind. What do you achieve day by day?

(After a pause Dogen said:) Buddha ancestors' body and mind are timelessness. Your true face is a great jewel forming in heaven. How long have you awaited timelessness? This auspicious day knows the increasing light of opportunity.

[Shakyamuni Buddha's enlightenment ceremony, the eighth day of the twelfth month]

At night amid the withered grass, after practicing for six years, a monk thoughtlessly drifts among the plum blossoms.

A spring wind rises. Red-and-white branches are proud of themselves. Senior monks, do you want to know the cause of Monk Gautama's* enlightenment? One: Hearing Tiantong's words of dropping off, I attained the buddha way. Two: Using my fist, I, Daibutsu,* enter your eyeballs. With miraculous wisdom the buddha transforms sentient beings. Seeing the morning star all of a sudden, he steals your entire body while sitting on the diamond seat.

Grasping and letting go is clearly one activity, encountering thirty-three generations of Indian and Chinese ancestors all at once. So, how is the World-honored One's life root in your own hands? Do you still want to meet the World-honored One?

(Dogen raised his fist for a while, then spread his five fingers and continued to speak:) You all have just met the World-honored One. After having met him, how is it?

(Dogen paused for a while and continued:) At the very moment of attaining enlightenment upon seeing the morning star, this is where the Tathagatha eats his morning gruel.

[Cutting the Arm Ceremony, the tenth day of the twelfth month]

(After telling the story of Huike, the Second Chinese Ancestor, who stood in the snow and cut off his arm, Dogen said:) Seeing the winter snow last night and this morning, I, Eihei,* recall the ancient time of Huike at the Shaoxi Peak of Mt. Song. Deep feelings and tears fill my heart and wet my collar. In reverence to him, I now uphold buddha-dharma. Standing in the snow and cutting off an arm is not truly difficult. I only regret that we do not have such a master now. I encourage you to aspire to the ancient practice.

Snow and more snow, one thousand, ten thousand miles,
flakes after flakes, not the same, not different.

Seeking song, seeking dance, the universe is new.
Burying the moon, burying the clouds, the fire pit vanishes.
Five petals and six blossoms accord with time, accord with
 season.
Not fearing winter's freezing and the year's cold end,
the valley pine and mountain bamboo speak with an empty
 heart.

[New Year's Eve, the twenty-eighth day of the twelfth month]

(After thanking the officers, the crew leaders, and the entire community, Dogen said:) With aspiration for enlightenment, you enter the kitchen. With your nose in the air, you inhale the fragrance of cooked rice. Carrying water and hauling firewood again and again, you begin to understand the great practice place at Eihei.

Now, I remember that a monk asked Zhaozhou,* "When two mirrors are facing each other, which one is clearer?" Zhaozhou said, "Your eyelid covers Mt. Sumeru.*"

If someone asked me the same question, I would respond: (Dogen raised his staff:) "What is this staff?" He may answer, "This is what I have learned on the meditation platform. But what is the way of going beyond buddha ancestors?"

(Dogen threw down the staff, descended from the dharma seat and said:) "I bow to you and say farewell."

[New Year's Day, morning]

On the morning of this auspicious day, I rejoice in zazen.
This monk's practice is steady as usual.
People wear their joyful New Year faces.
Nostrils and eyes are right here.
Pure white snow covers the river.
Fully content, Xie [Xuansha Shibei] fishes from his boat.

[The first full moon of the year, the fifteenth day of the first month]

Embodying myriad virtues,
cushions and ladles are profound.
Chairs merge with bamboo and wood.
Take up what is crystal clear,
then a thousand gaps and myriad distinctions become
    evident.
Let go and flow like water.
Ten directions, three times, bright and clear.
Tell me! What kind of practice can get at it?
Investigate this thoroughly.

(After a pause, Dogen said:)
The pure white wind of the house—plum blossoms, snow,
    and moon.
Fortunately there is a way of protecting our body at the time
    of flowering.
Clouds are clear, water is joyful, our effort is fulfilled.
Before we know it, our entire body enters the mystic village.

[Nirvana Ceremony, the fifteenth day of the second month]

The pairs of shala trees* do not need help from the Lord of
Spring.* After it snows, how do you know the frost of midnight?
The Tathagata turns the sky upside down and lays the world on
its side. From the white tuft between his eyebrows, the Tathagata
shines his light twice. Although it actually happened, who says
that he lost his life or that he didn't care about letting go while
sitting, or perishing while standing? The Seven Original Buddhas' bowls are bottomless. The calamities of sentient beings are
groundless.

If you call what happened on this day pari-nirvana, you are
not his disciple. If you call it not pari-nirvana, your words have
not hit the mark. Today has come and how is it? Do you want to
see the life vein of the Tathagata? Offer incense, make bows, and
return to the monks' hall.

[Closing the furnace, the first day of the third month]

A painted circle has come around to spring.
Opening and closing in accord with the season
is like the act of painting.
Place charcoal, look at the ash, and add snow.
I call it a red furnace.

[Bathing the Buddha Ceremony, the eighth day of the fourth month]

Our Buddha Tathagata was born on this day. He took seven steps in ten directions all at once. Who knows that buddhas were born at each of his steps? Buddhas have transmitted the voice of this day person to person. Past, present, and future—same birth, same place, same name. Homage to Shakyamuni Buddha. Elder brothers, let me bathe your heads with scented water. This is the meaning of bathing the baby Buddha. What is bathing? Our Buddha has bathed all monks for a long time. Today, the assembly of monks bathes our Buddha.

(After a pause, Dogen said:) Great assembly, let's go to the buddha hall and bathe our Buddha.

[Starting the summer practice period,
the fifteenth day of the fourth month, day of full moon]

(On the first day of the summer practice period, Dogen ascended the teaching seat, held up a whisk, drew a circle in the air, and said:) Our peaceful dwelling, this practice period, goes beyond this.

(He drew another circle and said:) Peaceful dwelling is to study this thoroughly. So, it is taught that the buddha who is King of the Empty Eon received this life vein, becoming a buddha, becoming an ancestor. The fist and the staff embody this point. They transmit dharma and transmit the robe.

During each summer practice period, make each moment the

top of your head. Don't regard this as the beginning. Don't regard this as going beyond. Even if you see it as the beginning, kick it away. Even if you see it as going beyond, stomp on it. Then, you are not bound by beginning or going beyond. How is it?

(Dogen took up the whisk, drew a circle, and said:) Dwell peacefully in this nest.

[The Tango Ceremony*—the fifth day of the fifth month]

Today is our festival of the big sky, the fifth day of the fifth month.
Samantabhadra and Manjushri act like worldly fellows.
Taking up a sixteen-foot stalk of grass,*
I tend Guishan's water buffalo.*

[Due to the fierce summer heat and humidity,
the first day of the sixth month—in the middle of the practice
period—is the time to end formal zazen.]

This morning, the first day of the sixth month, we stop sitting zazen and cease striking the board. But even in the peak heat of summer, don't throw away that old Zen board. Just remember to transmit dharma and save sentient beings.

[End of the summer practice period, the fifteenth day of the seventh
month, day of the full moon, completion of the dharma year]

The manifestation of ancient and present bodies awakens beings. Those who manifest Baizhang's* body, Linji's body, Old Man Shakyamuni's body, or the great master Bodhidharma's body, all expound dharma. Those who manifest the timeless ancient body expound dharma by actualizing the timeless ancient body. Those who manifest the timeless present body, expound dharma by actualizing the timeless present body. This summer brings forth undivided activity. The ancient summer brings forth undivided activity. This being so, our ninety-day peaceful dwelling has been a time of great fortune, great auspiciousness. As this peaceful dwelling is completed, is its merit large or small?

(Dogen paused for some time and said:) For sentient beings here on earth, the more dirt there is, the larger the buddha can be.

[The harvest moon in midautumn, the fifteenth day of the eighth month. An interim period continues before a scheduled practice in the monastery takes place.]

Who says the fan and the mirror are both incomplete?
This evening we all happen to see the whole circle.
In the ocean of a billion worlds, no moment can be measured.
The begging bowl's mouth faces the heavens.

Glossary of Terms

In the following entries, C. = Chinese, J. = Japanese, and S. = Sanskrit origins of terms.

abbot: J., *dōchō,* literally meaning "head of the hall." Also, *jūji* or *jūjinin,* meaning "one who abides in and maintains." The spiritual leader and administrative chief of a Zen monastery. (Later, in large Japanese monasteries, the administrative function became independent from the abbotship.)

acquired enlightenment: J., *shikaku.* Enlightenment attained by becoming free of delusion. Also translated as *initial enlightenment.*

administrator: J., *kan'in, inju,* or *kusu.* The equivalent of director, assistant director, and treasurer combined. Also translated as *monastery administrator.*

ancestor: An earlier teacher of the dharma lineage.

arhat: (S.) A follower of the Buddha's path who has attained personal nirvāna, literally meaning worthy or venerable. See *four fruits of attainment.*

attaining the way: J., *jōdō. Jō* means "becoming" or "completing." *Dō* in this case is a translation of Sanskrit *bodhi* (enlightenment).

Basically indicating Shākyamuni Buddha's enlightenment under the bodhi tree.

attendant monk: J., *jisha.* A monk high in seniority who works for the abbot as a secretary, and sometimes also as an assistant teacher.

attendant worker: J., *anja.* One who serves as a personal assistant to a Zen teacher.

auxiliary cloud hall: J., *jūundō.* A hall for zazen, eating, and sleeping, attached to the main monks' hall. Zen monks are known as clouds and water, for they move about freely with no permanent abode.

backward step: See *take the backward step and turn the light inward.*

beads: J., *juzu.* Literally meaning "jewels for counting." Most commonly consisting of 108 beads for subduing that many types of delusions. Used in some schools for counting mantras or prostrations.

beyond thinking: J., *hishirō.* See *nonthinking.*

beyondness: J., *ichinyo.* Literally meaning "one thusness." A state of being beyond dualism.

billion worlds: See *sahā worlds.*

birth and death: J., *shōji.* 1. The ongoing cycle of birth, death, and rebirth, which in Buddhism is viewed as suffering. See also *twelve-fold causation of rebirth.* 2. Life viewed as a continuous occurrence of birth and death moment by moment. 3. Birth as a complete, independent experience in the present moment without reference to other moments; death in the same manner.

blind one: One who experiences nonduality.

blood vein: Continuation of the dharma and precept lineage.

bodhi: (S.) J., *budai.* Awakening, enlightenment.

bodhi tree: See *attaining the way.*

bodhisattva: See *bodhisattva-māhasattva.*

bodhisattva-mahāsattva: (S.) Literally meaning "enlightened being, great being." One dedicated to enlightenment, who vows to bring others across to the shore of enlightenment before resting there. A future buddha. This term can also be translated as "enlightened beings and great beings."

bodhisattvas of the ten stages and three classes: Bodhisattvas are classified into the forty-two degrees according to their maturity. The first thirty degrees are called three classes. The more advanced ten degrees are called the ten stages or the ten grounds. That makes forty degrees. There are yet two more stages to go in order to be equal to a buddha.

body-mind of itself will drop away: One becomes free of the sense of boundary of the self.

bowing cloth: J., *zagu.* A patched cloth spread fully or folded in three or four on the floor or bowing mat for bowing on it. It is folded and carried around a forearm under the robe when not spread during a ceremony.

bowing mat: J., *haiseki.* A straw mat spread in front of the altar, on which the officiate of a ceremony makes a full bow to the enshrined image.

buddha: (S.) An awakened one.

Buddha: (S.) Usually referring to Shākyamuni Buddha.

buddha ancestors: Earlier awakened teachers of the dharma lineage.

buddha body: S., *buddhakāya.* J., *busshin.* Three bodies or aspects of buddha: 1. *dharmakāya* (*hosshin*):—dharma or indescribable body, absolute aspect of truth, equal to the whole phenomenal universe. 2. *sambhogakāya* (*hōjin*):—reward, enjoyment, bliss, or purified body, associated with the fruit of practice. 3. *nirmānakāya* (*ōjin*):—manifestation body that appears in the world and acts for the benefit of beings. The buddha body that has these three aspects is also known as the true human body (J., *shinjitsu nintai*).

buddha-dharma: (S.) Truth taught by a buddha; reality experienced by an awakened one.

buddha mind seal: See *buddha seal.*

buddha seal: J., *butchin.* Unchanging reality experienced by a buddha. Also, recognition of the buddha mind and entrustment of the teaching. Same as *buddha mind seal.*

Buddha's birthday: Shākyamuni Buddha's birthday is traditionally celebrated on the eighth day of the fourth month in East Asia.

cabinet for bedding: J., *kanki.* A cabinet in the back of each *tan* in the monks' hall for storing bedding and personal items.

carriages: See *officially not allowing a needle, but unofficially permitting carriages and horses to pass.*

counting grains of sand: Interpreting innumerable letters of scripture.

countless hands and eyes: Referring to one thousand arms and one thousand eyes of Bodhisattva Avalokiteshvara.

darkness: Also, night, which often represents the realm of nondifferentialtion; or else nonduality.

dead ash: Sitting in stillness.

deva: A celestial being, in the highest of the six paths of transmigration.

Deva Vehicle: The teaching for celestial beings. See *Five Vehicles.*

dharma: (S.) Ultimate reality; the Buddha's teaching of it; a thing or phenomenon.

dharma body: See *buddha body.*

dharma gate: J., *hōmon.* Entrance to teaching. Teaching of dharma.

dharma hall: One of the main buildings of a monastery, where formal dharma talks are given.

Dharma King: Shākyamuni Buddha.

dharma transmission: Acknowledgment of mastery and entrustment of buddha dharma from teacher to disciple (J., *dempō*), also the inheritance of it (*shihō*).

dharma wheel: J., *hōrin.* The full, continuous, and dynamic teaching of the Buddha. The "wheel" is a symbol of a monarch in ancient India, representing justice and the crushing of hindrances.

dharmakāya: See *buddha body.*

dhyāna: (S.) C., *chan.* J., transliterated as *Zen,* translated as *jōryo.* Meditation. One of the six pāramitās or realizations.

diamond seat: J., *kongōza.* The name for the seat beneath the bodhi tree where Shākyamuni Buddha was sitting when he attained enlightenment.

dōan: (J.) Assistant to *ino,* whose work includes sounding bells and drums during chanting.

dragon: Often represents an enlightened person. Same as *true dragon.*

dragon song: Fresh, joyous, and vast awareness.

drop away: J., *datsuraku.* To experience complete freedom beyond delusion and enlightenment, with nonattachment to body and mind.

eight virtues: See *water with eight virtues.*

eighteen sense realms: J., *jūhakkai.* eyes, ears, nose, tongue, body, mind; form, sound, smell, taste, touches, object of mind; eye consciousness, ear consciousness, nose consciousness, tongue consciousness, body consciousness, mind consciousness.

Empty Eon: J., *Kūgō.* The four stages in a world cycle are: becoming, abiding, decaying, and empty. The buddha who appears in the Empty Eon is called the King of the Empty Eon *(Ion Ō)* or King of Emptiness *(Kū Ō)*, and is regarded as a symbol of the original reality.

enlightenment: J., *go, satori.* Fundamental awareness of reality beyond dualism. Also, realization or experience of reality.

entrance screen: J., *ren.* A summer screen made of fine bamboo sticks, and a winter screen made of cloth.

eye: Often represents awakening.

eyeball: J., *ganzei.* That which represents true seeing, or understanding; hence buddha ancestors. Also, essence.

five skandhas: J, *goon, goun.* The five aggregates or streams of all physical and mental elements in the phenomenal world: form (matter), feeling, perception, impulses or volition, and discernment. What is commonly seen as a self is explained as an interdependent combining of these elements, not a fixed entity performing various functions.

Five Vehicles: J., *gojō.* Three Vehicles plus Human Vehicle and Deva Vehicle.

forming cloud, forming water: "Cloud (and) water" usually refers to a monk, who often wanders around in search of the way.

four bodily presences: J., *shigi.* The noble forms in everyday life: walking, standing, sitting, and lying down.

four fruits of attainment: Achievements of a practitioner as: a stream-enterer who has become free from delusions; once-returner and never-returner who have become free from desires; one who has no more need to study; and one who is worthy of offering. The last stage is called the fruit of being an arhat.

four great elements: Earth, water, fire, and air.

four types of beings: Those who come to existence by *four types of birth.*

four types of birth: Womb birth, egg birth, moisture birth (such as a worm), and transformation birth (such as birth into a deva resulted by karma).

four types of humans and celestial practitioners: J., *ninden shishu.* Monks, nuns, laymen, and laywomen of buddha-dharma. Devas or celestial beings are often seen as practicing together with humans.

full-lotus posture: J., *kekka fuza.* Sitting with both legs crossed over each other.

fundamental enlightenment: J., *hongaku.* Enlightenment that is intrinsic to each person, that is actualized by practice. Also translated as *original enlightenment.*

fundamental point: See *kōan.*

gasshō: (J.) Putting palms together in front of the chest. A form of expressing respect.

go into the mud and enter the weeds: To go into the common world for offering guidance.

gourd: Twining vine, or succession of the dharma lineage.

great enlightenment: Enlightenment without a trace of it.

Great Vehicle: S., *Mahāyāna,* a later development of Buddhism, centering on the teaching of bodhisattvas who are committed to awaken others. See also *Lesser Vehicles.*

greeting circuit: J., *jundō.* The abbot or practice leader goes around inside the monks' hall to greet all practitioners.

groping for a pillow: See *hand is reaching back, groping for a pillow.*

growing horn on the head: Experiencing formless form.

guest and host: J., *hinju.* Student and teacher.

guest manager: J., *shika.* One of the six officers of the monastery.

Guishan's water buffalo: Guishan Liangjue taught the assembly: "After I have passed away I will become a water buffalo at the foot of this mountain. On the left side of the buffalo's chest the characters, 'I am a monk of Guishan' will be written. When you call me the monk of Guishan, I will be a water buffalo. When you call me water buffalo, I will be a monk of Guishan. Now, how are you going to call me?"

half-lotus posture: J., *hanka fuza.* Sitting with one leg crossed on the other.

hall of light: J., *shōdō.* See *study hall.*

han: (J.) A hanging wooden board struck by a wooden mallet as a signal in a monastery.

hand reaches back, groping for a pillow: Meditative state of non-thinking.

head monk: See *shuso.*

Hīnayāna: (S.) J., *shōjō.* See *Three Vehicles.*

home-leavers: J., *shukke.* Monks and/or nuns.

horses: See *officially not allowing a needle, but officially permitting carriages and horses to pass.*

hōsan: (J.) The day of rest from scheduled monastic activities. Also meaning the end of a day's zazen.

incarnate body: J., *keshin.* A buddha body attained by miraculous power.

initial enlightenment: See *acquired enlightenment.*

ino: (J.) An officer in charge of activities in the monks' hall and ceremonies. One of the six main officers of the monastery.

isshu: (J.) The right hand covers the left fist on chest for walking meditation or mindful walking. Nowadays, also means *shashu.*

just sitting: J., *shikan taza.* Practice of zazen with no attempt to solve questions. Sometimes referred to in contrast with kōan studies.

just this: J., *immo.* Reality itself that cannot be grasped or named.

kalpa: (S.) Eon, an incalculable span of time.

karma: (S.) Action, or effect of action.

kashāya: (S.) J., *kesa* (or *okesa*, an honorific Japanese spoken expression). A patched robe worn over one shoulder by a Buddhist monk or nun. Represents a monk or nun.

kōan: (J.) An exemplary story, words, or encounter dialogue of an ancient master pointing to realization, to be studied and experienced by a Zen student under the guidance of the teacher. Also, for Dōgen, the fundamental point, or truth which is experienced directly.

Lesser Vehicles: J., *nijō*. See *Three Vehicles*.

light inward: See *take the backward step and turn the light inward*.

lion roaring: Vibrant awareness.

Lose (their) lives: To become free from ones' limited selves.

Mahāyāna: See *Great Vehicle*.

mantra: (S.) J., *shingon*, or *ju*. Literally, "true word"; "magical spell." Indicates a dhārāni, especially a short one. The sound is not necessarily translatable, but it has a specific psychospiritual effect.

marrow: See *You have attained my marrow*.

mind-ground: J., *shinchi*. Foundation of all things, sometimes called mind-nature or mind-field. Limitless mind that is identical with all things.

Mind itself is buddha: J., *sokushin zebutsu*. The teaching that individual consciousness is not separate from buddha mind.

mind seal: Confirmation of the merging of the minds of teacher and disciple. See also *buddha seal*.

monastery administrator: See *administrator*.

monks' hall: J., *sōdō, undō*. One of the main buildings of a Zen monastery, where monks reside, engage in zazen, and take morning and midday meals.

muddy water: Delusion.

mudrā: (S.) Seal, shape, or proof. The symbol of a buddha or bodhisattva's original vow. Also a physical gesture or posture.

nets and baskets: J., *rarō.* Bird nets and fish-catching baskets. Being confined by delusion.

night period: J., *kō.* One-fifth of the time from sunset to sunrise.

nirmānakāya: J., *ōjin.* Mmanifestation body that appears in the world and acts for the benefit of beings.

nirvāna: (S.) Literally, "putting out fire." The state of freedom from desire, dualistic thought, and suffering in the chain of rebirth. Also means *pari-nirvāna.*

nondefilement: J., *fuzenna.* Freedom from duality. Also translated as *nondividedness.*

nondividednes: J., *fuzenna.* Also translated as *nondefilement.*

nonmerging: J., *fuego.* No more merging in complete merging of realization.

nonthinking: J., *hishiryō.* In contrast to "thinking" *(shiryō)* and "not thinking" *(fushiryō),* "nonthinking" describes the unrestricted mind in zazen in which one tries neither to develop nor to suppress thoughts which are continually arising. These terms come from the following dialogue: When Yaoshan was sitting, a monk asked him, "In steadfast sitting, what do you think?" Yaoshan said, "Think not thinking." "How do you think not thinking?" Yaoshan replied, "Nonthinking." Also translated as *beyond thinking.*

nostrils: J., *bikū.* That which is essential. Same as original face, eyeball, bones, and marrow.

ocean drying up: Still, much water is left and its bottom is not yet seen. Sitting in stillness.

officers: J., *chiji.* See *six officers.*

officially not allowing a needle, but unofficially permitting carriages and horses to pass: The experience [of ocean mudra samadhi] at each moment may seem partial and incomplete but it is full and complete.

one billion worlds: S., *trichilocosm.* J., *sanzen sekai, sanzen daisen sekai.* The entire cosmos. See *sahā worlds.*

one bright pearl: Complete and nondual reality.

one hundred grasses: Infinite phenomena.

original enlightenment: See *fundamental enlightenment.*

original face: Buddha nature, or compete and nondual reality, inherent to each person.

original realization: J., *honshō.* See *fundamental enlightenment.*

pari-nirvāna: (S.) The Buddha's great death.

practice: J., *shu, shū, shugyō, gyō.* Activities centered around zazen. A continuous process of actualizing enlightenment, according to Dōgen.

practice and realization/practice-enlightenment: J., *shushō.* See *practice within realization.*

practice period: J., *ango.* Literally, "peaceful dwelling." A three-month period of intensive practice. In Dōgen's time the summer practice period ran from the fifteenth day of the fourth month to the fifteenth day of the seventh month. It actually consisted of eighty-five days, but is rounded up as customary in East Asia, and was called a ninety-day practice period. (The winter practice period, which ran from the fifteenth day of the tenth month to the fifteenth day of the first month, was also traditional. But for Dōgen, practice period meant summer practice period.)

practice within realization: J., *shōjō no shu.* Literally, "realization on top of practice." Practice which is inseparable from enlightenment or realization of buddha nature.

practice-realization: See *practice within realization.*

prajñā: (S.) J., *hannya, chie.* Wisdom to see directly beyond dualistic views. Wisdom beyond wisdom.

prajñā pāramitā: Arriving at *prajñā*, or realization of wisdom beyond wisdom. Six pāramitās are: giving, ethical conduct, patience, enthusiasm, meditation, and prajñā.

receptive samādhi: J., *jijuyū zammai.* Also known as self-fulfilling samādhi. The buddha's realizing and utilizing the joy of samādhi. Sometimes contrasted to *tajiyū zammai*—the aspect of extending samādhi, shared with other beings.

red heart: J., *sekishin.* Unadorned, selfless mind/heart.

reward body: See *buddha body.*

root teacher: J., *honshi.* One who has ordained or given dharma transmission to the student.

Sacred Monk: The statue enshrined in the center of the monks' hall. Most commonly that of Mañjushrī Bodhisattva.

sahā worlds: The cosmos within the reach of Shākyamuni Buddha's teaching. "*Sahā*" (S.) means endurance, referring to the hardship of its inhabitants, which requires the development of patience. Sūtras say that there are a billion such worlds, each consisting of Mt. Sumeru and the Four Continents that surround it.

samādhi: (S.) J., *sammai, zammai* (transliterations). A one-pointed, stable state of meditation. Sometimes translated as *jō* or stability.

sambhogakāya: See *buddha body.*

sea of birth and death: A cycle of transmigration seen as continuous suffering. A way toward the shore of enlightenment.

seal: See *buddha seal, mudrā.*

secretary: J., *shoki.* Scribe in a monastery.

semiformal bows: J., *sokurei.* The bower folds the bowing cloth in four, puts it on the floor, and touches it with the forehead. See *spreading the cloth twice.*

sense realms: See *eighteen sense realms.*

sentient beings: Living beings, including humans. Sometimes indicates those who are not awakened.

sewn inside the robe: A story in the *Lotus Sūtra*: A man went to see a dear friend, got drunk, and fell asleep. The friend who was going on a long official journey sewed a priceless pearl inside his robe as a gift. But the man never noticed it.

shāla trees: Four pairs of fragrant giant trees standing in the four directions around the Buddha's bed at the time of his parinirvāna.

shashu: (J.) A mindful way of holding hands on the chest. One hand covers the other hand, which is closed in a fist. In the traditional Chinese way, the left hand covers the right fist. The current Sōtō way is the reverse other way. See also *isshu.*

short dharma body: A particular manifestation of reality itself.

shuso: (J.) Literally meaning "head seat." One who assists the abbot in teaching during the practice period as part of their training.

single great matter: J., *ichidaiji.* Realizing the true dharma.

six officers: J., *roku chiji.* The six main officers of a monastery are: *tsūsu,* director; *kansu,* assistant director; *fūsu,* treasurer; *ino,* supervisor of practice for the monks; *tenzo,* head cook; and *shissui,* work leader.

six paths: The "roads" in the cycle of birth, death, and rebirth: worlds of hell beings, hungry ghosts, animals, fighting spirits, humans, and devas. The first four are regarded as unwholesome and the last two as wholesome.

sixteen-foot stalk of grass: Based on Yuanwu Keqin's words in the *Blue Cliff Record,* Case 8: "At one time take up a stalk of grass and turn it into a golden sixteen-foot body of the Buddha. At another time take up a golden sixteen-foot body of the Buddha and turn it into a stalk of grass."

skillful means: S., *upāya.* J., *hōben.* Expedient methods to remove deluded people's doubts and lead them to realize true dharma.

skin bag: A human or animal.

skin dropping off completely: Experiencing freedom from the confinement of the self.

skull: Sitting in stillness.

Small Vehicles: J., *shōjō*. See *Three Vehicles*.

soul: J., *reichi*. An everlasting identity throughout a series of transmigrations. Dōgen denies existence of such a permanent self.

south of Xiang, north of Tan: Both Xiang and Tan are situated near Changsha (Hunan Province). Meaning in the same place or anywhere.

splattered by mud and soaked in water: Identifying with sentient beings in guiding them.

spreading the bowing cloth twice: J., *saiten*. Used for a greeting. The bower spreads the bowing cloth with two folds on the floor, picks it up without bowing, folds it the long way, puts it around one arm (in the carrying position), delivers a greeting statement, and makes three semiformal bows. See *semiformal bows*.

spring: Often meaning total experience of the world.

standing bow: J., *monjin*. Literally meaning inquiring or greeting. Bowing with hands together in front of the chest while standing.

study hall: J., *shuryō*. A building in the Zen monastery where monks read, drink tea, and have evening meals. Also called *hall of light*.

supernatural powers: J., *jinzū shushō*. Practice and realization of such extraordinary abilities as five miraculous powers—insight into others' minds, the celestial eye, the celestial ear, knowing the past, and removing misery.

sūtra: (S.) J., *kyō*. Literally, warp as in weaving, later meaning principle of the teaching. Now refers to Indian Buddhist scriptures that take the form of a discourse by Buddha as heard and verified by one of his disciples.

take the backward step and turn the light inward: J., *ekō henshō no taiho wo mochiiru.* Stop moving forward in daily activities and reflect with attention inward on essential practice of zazen.

tall dharma body: A particular manifestation of reality itself.

tan: (J.) A platform in the monks' hall with assigned places for zazen and formal morning and midday meals, as well as for sleeping.

Tango Ceremony: The fifth day of the fifth month, a day of celebration for boys. One of the traditional East Asian holidays, along with the first day of the first month, the third day of the third month, the seventh day of the seventh month, and the ninth day of the ninth month.

tathāgata: A buddha.

Tathāgata: (S.) An honorific name for the Buddha, meaning the one who comes thus, or who has come from thusness.

ten directions: North, south, east, west, their midpoints, plus up and down.

ten stages: See *bodhisattvas of ten stages and three classes.*

tenzo: Head of the kitchen in a Zen monastery; one of the six officers.

three classes: See *bodhisattvas of ten stages and three classes.*

three learnings: J., *sangaku.* Study and practice of precepts, samādhi, and prajñā.

three lower paths: Worlds of animals, hungry ghosts, and hell beings.

three realms: J., *sangai.* 1. desire realm, including the six paths. 2. form realm of those who are free from desire. 3. formless realm of those who have attained the highest worldly mental states through meditative exercises.

three times: The present lifetime, the next lifetime, and subsequent lifetimes. Also meaning past, present, and future.

Three Vehicles: J., *sanjō.* According to the traditional Mahāyāna Buddhist view, the Buddha's teaching is classified into the three ways to move from the ocean of birth and death to the shore of enlightenment: The Shrāvaka (listener) Vehicle, the Pratyeka-buddha (solitary awakened being) Vehicle, and the Great Vehicle. The first two are called the Hīnayāna, Two Vehicles, or Lesser (Small) Vehicle(s). The Great Vehicle (Mahāyāna), which emphasizes bringing all sentient beings to enlightenment, is also called the Bodhisattva Vehicle.

thusness: Reality as it is, things as they are.

treasury of the true dharma eye: Once Shākyamuni Buddha, at an assembly on Vulture Peak, took up an udumbara flower and winked. Mahākāshyapa smiled. Then, Shākyamuni Buddha said, "I have the treasury of the true dharma eye, the inconceivable heart of nirvāna. This I entrust to Mahākāshyapa."

true dragon: See *dragon.*

turn the light inward: See *take the backward step and turn the light inward.*

turning point: A place where delusion is transformed into enlightenment.

turning the (great) dharma wheel: The Buddha expounding dharma. See also *dharma wheel.*

turning the body in the word vein: Being free from intellectual, verbal thinking.

turning the great dharma wheel: The Buddha expounding dharma. See also *dharma wheel.*

twelve hours: J., *jūni ji.* In East Asia a day was divided into twelve hours: six for daytime and six for nighttime. See the diagram on p. 110. "Twelve hours" also means ordinary time or secular world.

twelve-fold causation of rebirth: J., *jūni rinden, jūni innen.* The chain of the "dependent origination" (*innen*) of pain and despair in the cycle of birth, death, and rebirth: ignorance, karma-formations, consciousness, name-and-form (corporeality), six sense-fields (the spheres of sense activities), contact, feeling (sensation), craving (thirst), grasping (clinging), becoming (action), birth (rebirth), and decay (old age, sickness) and death. The logical formula is as follows: "Ignorance is the cause of karma-formations. Karma-formations are the cause of consciousness," and so on to decay and death.

Twenty-five existences: J., *nijūgo u.* Types of beings in the three realms: fourteen in the desire realm, seven in the form realm, and four in the formless realm.

Two Lesser Vehicles: J., *nijō.* See *Three Vehicles.*

umpan: (J.) Literally meaning "cloud board." A metal board in the shape of rising cloud, hung in the kitchen or the study hall for sounding signals.

unfolding the stillness: J., *kaijō.* Leaving the seat after the end of a zazen period.

water with eight virtues: Water in the Seven Seas around Mt. Sumeru or lakes in paradise is said to be sweet, chill, soft, light, pure, no smelling, gentle on throat, and gentle on stomach.

way: See *attaining the way.*

way-seeking mind: S., *bodhicitta.* J., *dōshin.* The mind that pursues the supreme realization. Same as thought of enlightenment, aspiration for enlightenment.

weeds: Delusions or the world of delusions.

withered tree: Sitting in stillness.

work leader: See *six officers.*

World-honored One: Shākyamuni Buddha.

You have attained my marrow: Skin, flesh, bones, marrow—each represents the essence of teaching. Bodhidharma's words to his students.

zafu: (J.) A round cushion placed under the buttocks during zazen.

zazen: (J.) Meditation in a seated posture. A compound of *za* (sitting) and *Zen* (meditation). Total concentration of body and mind in upright sitting position, which is the basis of Zen Buddhist practice.

Zen: (J.) A transliteration of *dhyāna* (S.) and *chan* (C.), meaning meditation. Also, Zen School of Buddhism and the Zen Buddhist way of understanding.

Names of persons, deities, Buddhist schools, books, and some places mentioned in the main text are briefly explained here. The Japanese versions of names are shown in brackets. Chinese provinces are parenthesized. The dates are CE (AD) unless otherwise specified.

Ājñātakaundinya: The one who was enlightened first among the five earliest disciples of Shākyamuni Buddha.

Ānanda: A disciple and cousin of Shākyamuni Buddha. Known as the foremost learner of the Buddha's teaching, who remembered and narrated the sūtras after the Buddha's death. Regarded as the dharma heir of Mahākāshyapa and as the Second Ancestor in the Zen tradition.

Avatamsaka School: C., *Huayanzong. [Kegonshū].* Established by Fazang [Hōzō], it flourished during the Tang Dynasty (618–907) along with the Tiantai School before the Zen School became dominant in China. Provided a theoretical background for much of Zen thought. The teaching is based on the principle in the *Avatamsaka Sūtra* that all things interacting with one another without obstruction. As the Kegon

School in Japan it became one of the six schools of Buddhism in the Nara Period (710–794).

Baizhang Huaihai: [Hyakujō Ekai]. 749–814, China. A dharma heir of Mazu Daoyi *[Baso Dōitsu]*, Nanyue Line. Founder of the Dazhi Shousheng Monastery, Mt. Baizhang, Hong Region (Jiangxi). Known as the initiator of monastic regulations for Chinese Zen, and famed for many sayings and dialogues.

Bodhidharma: [*Bodaidaruma*]. Ca. fifth to sixth centuries. Brought Zen teaching from India to China. Regarded as the Twenty-eighth Indian Ancestor and the First Chinese Ancestor. According to legend, he arrived in the southern Chinese kingdom of Liang in 527 and had a dialogue with Emperor Wu. Then he went to the northern kingdom of Wei and sat facing the wall for nine years at the Shaolin Temple, Mt. Song (Henan). Daoyu, Huike, nun Zongchi, and Daofu are known as his disciples.

Butsuju Myōzen: 1184–1225, Japan. A dharma heir of Myōan Eisai. As abbot of the Kennin Monastery, Kyōto, he taught Rinzai Zen to Dōgen. He went with Dōgen to China but died at the Tiantong Monastery during their study.

Caodong School: The dharma lineage derived from Dongshan. One of the Five Schools of Zen in China. Dōgen brought this teaching and is regarded as founder of its Japanese form, the Sōto School.

Caoshan Benji: [Sōzan Honjaku]. 840–901, China. A dharma heir of Dongshan Liangjie. Sometimes regarded as a cofounder of the Caodong School along with Dongshan. Taught at Mt. Cao, Fu Region (Jiangxi). Posthumous name, Great Master Yuanzheng.

Complete Enlightenment Bodhisattva: One who receives the Buddha's teaching in the *Sūtra of Complete Enlightenment*.

Dai, Emperor: [Daisō]. An emperor of the Tang Dynasty, China. On throne 763–780.

Daibutsu: Dōgen called himself in this way when he resided at the Daibutsu Monastery.

Daibutsu Monastery: After moving to Echizen Province, Japan, in 1243, Dōgen founded this "Great Buddha" Monastery in the following year. Renamed Eihei Monastery two years later.

Dajian Huineng: [Daikan Enō]. 638–713. The legendary Sixth Chinese Ancestor of the Zen School. A dharma heir of the Fifth Ancestor Daman Hongren. Also called Laborer Lu. Taught at the Baolin Monastery, Mt. Caoxi, Shao Region (Guangdong). Regarded as founder of the Southern School of Zen. Posthumous name, Zen Master Dajian. Some of his dharma discourses are included in the *Sixth Ancestor's Platform Sūtra*.

Damei Fachang: [Daibai Hōjō]. 752–839, China. A dharma heir of Mazu Daoyi, Nanyue Line. After retreat of forty years, taught at Mt. Damei, Yin Prefecture (Zhejiang).

Dayi Daoxin: [Daii Dōshin]. 580–651. Fourth Ancestor of Chinese Zen. Dharma heir of Jianzhi Sengcan. Taught in Huangmei, Qi Region (Hubei). Posthumous name, Zen Master Dayi.

Dazu Huike: [Taiso Eka]. 487–593, China. A dharma heir of Bodhidharma. The Second Ancestor of Chinese Zen. Taught in the northern capital of Ye (Henan). Posthumous name, Great Master Zhengzong Pujue.

Dongshan Liangjie: [Tōzan Ryokai]. 807–869, China. A dharma heir of Yunyan Tansheng, Qingyuan Line. Taught at Mt. Dong, Ru Region (Jiangxi). Author of "Song of Precious Mirror Samādhi." Regarded as the founder of the Caodong School, one of the Five Schools of Chinese Zen.

Duofu: [Tafuku]. Ca. ninth century, China. A dharma heir of Zhaozhou Congshen, Nanyue Line. Taught in Hang Region (Zhejiang).

Eight Seas: See *Four Continents.*

Eihei: Dōgen called himself in this way after the Daibutsu Monastery was renamed Eihei (Eternal Peace) Monastery in 1246.

Eisai: See *Myōan Eisai.*

Ejō: See *Koun Ejō.*

Fang, Minister: [Bō Shōkoku]. Probably refers to Peixiu [Haikyū], 797–870, China, who studied with Huangbo Xiyun, in the Nanyue line, and edited Huangbo's *Essential Teaching of Transmission of Mind.*

Fayan School: The lineage of Fayan Wenyi [Hōgen Mon'eki] (885–958), Qingyuan Line. One of the Five Schools of Zen in China.

Feng, Minister: [Fū Shōkō]. d. 1153, China. A lay student of Fuyan Qingyuan [Butsugen Seion], Linji School.

Five Buddhas: [Gobutsu]. Mahāvairochana, Akshobhya, Ratnasambhava, Amitāyus (Amitābha), and Amoghasiddhi. Regarded as manifestations of the fivefold wisdom of Mahāvairochana in Vajrayāna (Esoteric) Buddhism.

Five Houses: The major schools of Chinese Zen after the late Tang Dynasty: The Guiyang, Linji, Caodong, Yunmen, and Fayan Schools.

Four Continents: According to sūtras, the world consists of Eight Seas among Nine Mountains that lie around Mt. Sumeru. Four continents lie in the Eight Seas. Among them, the Northern Continent, Uttarakuru, is where inhabitants live for one thousand years and don't know suffering. Therefore, they indulge in the pleasure of the present moment. The Southern Continent, Jambudvīpa, is where we humans live with suffering, but where we have the potential for awakening.

Gautama: [Kudon]. The family name in the Shākya Clan. Indicates Shākyamuni Buddha.

Gien: d. 1324, Japan. Formally a student of Ekan of the Japan Daruma School, he became Dōgen's student in 1241. A co-compiler of *The Extensive Record of Eihei.* The fourth abbot of the Eihei Monastery, succeeding Dōgen, Ejō, and Gikai.

Guidelines for Zen Monasteries: C., *Chanyuan Qinggui.* [Zennen Shingi]. Ten volumes. Compiled by Changlu Zongze [Chōro Sōsaku] (eleventh and twelfth centuries, China), Yunmen School. The oldest extant collection of monastic guidelines, as most of the earlier guidelines, attributed to Baizhang in legend, had been lost.

Guiyang School: [*Igyōshū*]. A lineage of Guishan Lingyou and his dharma heir Yangshan Huiji, Nanyue Line. One of the Five Schools of Zen in China.

Himālayas: Described in sūtras as the place where Shākyamuni Buddha practiced in his former life.

Hongzhi Zhengjue: [Wanshi Shōgaku]. 1091–1157, China. A dharma heir of Danxia Zichun [Tanka Shijin], Caodong School. As abbot at Mt. Tiantong his monastery flourished with as many as twelve hundred monks in residence. In a period when Zen practice was in decline, he revived the Cao-dong tradition. Regarded as leader of "silent-illumination Zen." Author of *Hongzhi's Capping Verses*, which became the basis of the *Book of Serenity*. Posthumous name, Zen Master Hongzhi.

Huangmei: A mountain in Qi Region (Hubei), China, where the Fifth Ancestor Daman Hongren [Daiman Kōnin] practiced zazen and taught.

Huike: See *Dazu Huike.*

Huineng: See *Dajian Huineng.*

Huizhong, National Teacher: See *Nanyang Huizhong.*

Indra: Originally a Hindu deity. Regarded in Buddhism as a main guardian deity of dharma. Resides in the Thirty-three Heav-ens above Mt. Sumeru.

Indra's Net Sūtra: A Mahāyāna sūtra, revered for its elucidation of the bodhisattva precepts.

Jambudvīpa: See *Four Continents.*

Jeta Grove: The place in the south of the city of Shrāvastī, in the Kaushala Kingdom, in northern India. According to sūtras, this is where Shākyamuni Buddha's community practiced together in the monastery during the rainy season.

Jiatai Record of the Universal Lamp: Jiatai Pudeng-lu [Katai Futōroku]. A Chinese record of the Zen tradition, including accounts on nuns and lay people, compiled by Leian Zhengshou [Raian Shōju] in the fourth year of Jiatai (1204).

Jingde Record of Transmission of the Lamp: Jingde Chuandeng-lu [Keitoku Dentōroku]. Compiled in the first year of Jingde Era (1004), China, probably by Yongan Daoyuan [Yōan Dōgen] of the Fayan School. A primary collection of words and deeds of 1,701 masters. A common Zen expression, "1,700 kōans," derived from this number.

Jingzhao Mihu: [Kyōchō Beiko]. Ca. ninth century, China. A dharma heir of Guishan Lingyou, Guiyang School. Biography not known.

Jingzhao Xiujing: [Keichō Kyūjō]. Ca. ninth century, China. A dharma heir of Dongshan Liangjie, founder of the Caodong School. Taught at the Jingzhao Huayan Monastery, Mt. Zhongnan, south of the city of Changan (Shanxi). Posthumous name, Great Master Baozhi.

Kāshyapa Buddha: One of the Seven Primordial Buddhas. Regarded as the mystic root teacher of Shākyamuni Buddha.

Keqin: See *Yuanwu Keqin.*

Kimmei, Emperor: On throne 510–570, Japan.

Kōshō (Hōrin) Monastery: Situated to south of Kyōto, Japan, founded by Dōgen in 1233. "Raising the Sages (Treasure Forest)" Monastery.

Koun Ejō: 1198–1280, Japan. After studying Zen with Kakuan of the Japan Daruma School, he became a student of Dōgen in 1234 and became the first head monk. As the most advanced student, he assisted Dōgen, edited many of his writings, and became his dharma heir. He was appointed the second abbot of the Eihei Monastery by Dōgen in 1253.

Li, Minister: [Ri Shōkoku]. Ca. ninth century, China. Studied Zen with Yaoshan Weiyan, Qingyuan line.

Linji School: The dharma lineage derived from Linji Yixuan, Nanyue Line. One of the Five Schools of Chinese Zen. Its Japanese form is the Rinzai School, of which Myōan Eisai is regarded as founder.

Linji Yixuan: [Rinzai Gigen]. d. 867, China. A dharma heir of Huangbo Xiyun [Ōbaku Kiun], Nanyue line. Taught at the Linji Monastery, Zhen Region (Hebei). Regarded as founder of the Linji School, one of the Five Schools of Chinese Zen. Posthumous name, Great Master Huizhao.

Lord of Spring: J., *tōkun.* Deity of the eastern direction, in charge of spring.

Longya Judun: [Ryūge Kodon] 835–923, China. A dharma heir of Dongshan Liangjie, Quingyuan line. Resided at Mt. Longya (Dragon Fang), (Hunan). Author of admonitions in verse for Zen practitioners.

Lotus School: See *Tiantai School.*

Magadha: An ancient kingdom in northern India, currently southern Bihar. Much of Shākyamuni Buddha's teaching activity took place in the region of its capital city, Rājagriha.

Mahākāshyapa: A senior disciple of Shākyamuni Buddha, who was engaged in ascetic practice. Regarded as the First Ancestor of the Zen School.

Maitreya: [Miroku]. Bodhisattva, Future Buddha. Predicted to come down from Tushita Heaven to the Continent of Jambudvīpa 5,670,000,000 years in the future, as the next Buddha, and awaken those who will have missed the teaching of Shākyamuni Buddha.

Mañjushrī: Bodhisattva of Wisdom, whose figure is often enshrined as the Sacred Monk in the center of the monks' hall in the Zen tradition.

Mantra School: [Shingonshū]. Esoteric Buddhist teaching, which was widely practiced but not organized as a school in China, was brought to Japan by Kūkai in 806, who soon established the Shingon School. "Mantra," literally meaning "true word," indicates dharma expressed in mystical syllables. The Shingon School, along with the Tendai School, was influential during Dōgen's time.

Mazu Daoyi: [Baso Dōitsu]. 709–788, China. A dharma heir of Nanyue Huairang, Nanyue line. Taught at the Kaiyuan Monastery, Zhongling (Jiangxi) with 139 enlightened disciples. Also called Jiangxi. Posthumous name, Zen Master Daji.

Mihu: See *Jingzhao Mihu.*

Mt. Huangmei: See *Huangmei.*

Mt. Sumeru: See *Four Continents.*

Myōan Eisai: 1141–1225, Japan. Studied Tendai and Esoteric (Tantric) practice at Mt. Hiei near Kyōto. On his second visit to China, he became a dharma heir of Xuan Huaichang [Kian Eshō] of the Linji School. Founded and taught Tendai studies, Esoteric Buddhism, and Zen at the Jufuku Monastery in Kamakura, and the Kennin Monastery in Kyōto. Regarded as founder of the Rinzai School.

Myōzen: See *Butsuju Myōzen.*

Nanyang Huizhong: [Nan'yō Echū]. d. 775, China. A dharma heir of the Sixth Ancestor Huineng. Taught at Nanyang (Hunan). Posthumous name, National Teacher Dazheng.

Nanyue Huairang: [Nangaku Ejō]. 677–744, China. A dharma heir of the Sixth Ancestor Huineng. Taught at the Bore

Monastery, Nanyue (Mt. Heng), Heng Region (Hunan). Regarded as founder of the Nanyue line. Posthumous name, Zen Master Dahui.

Nine Schools: [Kushū]. A classification of Buddhist schools: Kosha [Kusha] School, based on *Abhidharma-kosha Treatise* by Vasubandhu; Satyasiddhi [Jōjitsu] School, based on *Satyasiddhi Treatise* by Harivarman; Precept [Ritsu] School; Three Treatises [Sanron] School, based on Nāgārjuna's *Mādhyamika Treatise* and *Twelve Gate Treatise,* as well as Āryadeva's *One Hundred Treatises;* Tiantai [Tendai] School; Avatamsaka [Kegon] School; Dharma-lakshana [Hossō] School; Mantra [Shingon] School; and Zen School.

Puhua: [Fuke]. Ca. ninth century, China. Dharma heir of Panshan Baoji [Banzan Hōshaku], Nanyue line. Lived in Zhen Region (Hebei). A friend of Linji, he was known for outrageous conduct.

Qingfeng Chuanchu: [Seihō Denso] Ca. ninth century, China. A dharma heir of Luopu Yuanan [Rakuho Gen'an], Qingyuan line. Taught at Mt. Qingfeng (Shanxi).

Qingyuan Xingsi: [Seigen Gyōshi]. d. 740, China. A dharma heir of the Sixth Ancestor Huineng. Abbot of the Jingju Monastery, Mt. Qingyuan, Ji Region (Jiangxi). Regarded as founder of the Qingyuan line. Posthumous name, Great Master Hongji.

Rinzai School: See *Linji School.*

Rujing: See *Tiantong Rujing.*

Samantabhadra: [Fugen]. Bodhisattva of awakened practice in the world. This bodhisattva's image, along with Mañjushrī's, often accompanies that of Shākamuni Buddha.

Senika: [Senni]. A Brahman scholar described in the *Mahāparinirvāna Sūtra,* who asserted permanency of soul, but was argued down by Shākyamuni Buddha.

Senne: Ca. thirteenth century, Japan. As one of the senior disciples of Dōgen, he edited part of the *Extensive Record of Eihei* [Eihei Kōroku]. Author of *Verbatim Notes on Shōbōgenzō* [Shōbōgenzō Okikigaki], the earliest commentary on Dōgen's writings.

Seven Original/Primordial Buddhas: [Shichibutsu, Kako Shichibutsu]. Literally, the Seven Buddhas (of the Past). Includes six legendary buddhas from the immeasurable past through Kāshyapa Buddha, plus Shāyamuni Buddha.

Shākyamuni Buddha: [Shakamuni Butsu]. The founding teacher of Buddhism who lived in India around the fifth century BCE. In the Mahāyāna Buddhist tradition, his enlightenment as the awakening of all sentient beings is emphasized.

Shaolin Temple: Situated on Mt. Song (Henan), China, where Bodhidharma sat facing the wall for nine years.

Shun, Emperor: [Junsō]. An emperor of the Tang Dynasty China, reigning 805–807.

Shishuang Qingzhu: [Sekisō Keisho]. 807–888, China. A dharma heir of Daowu Yuanzhi [Dōgo Enchi], Qingyuan line. Taught at Mt. Shishuang, Tan Region (Hunan). Posthumous name, Great Master Puhui.

Sixin Wuxin: [Shishin Goshin]. 1043–1115, China. A dharma heir of Huitang Zuxin [Kaidō Soshin], Linji School. Taught at Mt. Huanglong, Nanchang Prefecture (Jiangxi).

Sumeru: (S.) [Shumi, Meiro]. See *Four Continents.*

Sushan Kuangren: [Sozan Kyōnin] Ca. ninth century, China. A dharma heir of Dongshan Liangjie. Taught at Mt. Su, Fu Region (Jiangxi).

Sūtra of the Three Thousand Guidelines for Pure Conducts (for Venerable Monks): [(Daibiku) Sanzen Igi Kyō]. A Mahāyāna sūtra on daily activities for home-leavers. Formally, the 250 precepts are called for in each of the four bodily presences in three times—past, present, and future.

Taibo Peak: See *Tiantong Rujing.*

Tan: See *south of Xiang, north of Tan* in the Glossary of Terms.

Tiantai School: C., *Tiantaizong.* [Tendaishū]. Established by
  Zhiyi [Chigi] at Mt. Tiantai, Tai Region (Zheijiang), China,
  in the sixth century. An all-encompassing school, based on
  Zhiyi's systematic classification of the entire canon. Central
  to this innovative, distinctively Chinese school are the *Lotus
  Sūtra* and the meditation practices of *shamatha* (Skt., ceasing
  of wavering mind) and *vipashyanā* (observation, understand-
  ing). Also called Lotus School. Along with Avatamsaka
  School, it flourished during the Tang Dynasty (618–907). Its
  Japanese form, the Tendai School, along with the Shingon
  School, was influential during Dōgen's time.

Tiantong Rujing: [Tendō Nyojō]. 1163–1228, China. A dharma
  heir of Xuedou Zhijian [Setchō Chikan], Caodong School.
  Taught at the Qingliang Monastery, Jiankang (Jiangsu); the
  Ruiyan Monastery, Tai Region (Zhejiang); and the Jingci
  Monastery, Hang Region (Zhejiang). In 1225 he became
  abbot of the Jingde Monastery, Mt. Tiantong (Mt. Taibo),
  Ming Region (Zhejiang), where he transmitted dharma to
  Dōgen.

Touzi Datong: [Tōsu Daidō]. 819–914, China. A dharma heir of
  Cuiwei Wuxue [Suibi Mugaku], Qingyuan Line. Taught at
  Mt. Touzi, Shu Region (Anhui). Posthumous name, Great
  Master Ciji.

Tushita Heaven: [Tosotsu Ten]. A "joyful" heaven in the desire
  realm (see *three realms* in the Glossary of Terms). This is be-
  lieved to be where bodhisattvas bound to become buddhas
  abide.

Vairochana: [Birushana, Biru]. Name for the dharmakāya buddha,
  literally, illumination. Mahāvairochana is the central deity of
  Esoteric Buddhism. Manifestation of reality of the universe.

Vajrasattva: [Kongō Satta]. A deity who conveys Vairochana's
  universal enlightenment to sentient beings who raise the

thought of enlightenment. Regarded as dharma heir of Vairochana and the Second Ancestor of Esoteric Buddhism.

Vimalakīrti: An enlightened layman who is the main figure of the *Vimalakīrti Sūtra.*

Vulture Peak: [Ryōju-sen]. S., *Gridhrakūta.* A mountain in the northeast of Rājagriha City, the capital of Magadha. Sūtras mention this as a place where Shākyamuni Buddha gave discourses.

Xiang: See *south of Xiang, north of Tan* in the Glossary of Terms.

Xiangyan Zhixian: [Kyōgen Chikan]. d. 898, China. A dharma heir of Guishan Lingyou, Guiyang School. Taught at the Xiangyan Monastery, Deng Region (Henan). Posthumous name, Great Master Xideng.

Xie: See *Xuansha Shibei.*

Xuansha Shibei: [Gensha Shibi]. 835–908, China. Third son of Xie Family. A dharma heir of Xuefeng Yicun, Qingyuan Line. Also called Ascetic Bei. Taught at the Xuansha Monastery, Fu Region (Fujian). Given title Great Master Zongyi by the Emperor.

Xuanze: See *Baoen Xuanze.*

Xuefeng Yicun: [Seppō Gison]. 822–908, China. A dharma heir of Deshan Xuanjian [Tokusan Senkan], Qingyuan Line. Taught at Mt. Xuefeng, Fu Region (Fujian). Posthumous name, Great Master Zhenjue.

Yaoshan Weiyan: [Yakusan Igen]. 745–828, China. A dharma heir of Shitou Xiquan [Sekitō Kisen], Qingyuan Line. Taught at Mt. Yao, Feng Region (Hunan). Posthumous name, Great Master Hongdao.

Yōmei, Emperor: On throne 585–587, Japan.

Yoshimine Temple: Also called Kippō Temple. Located in Echizen Province, Japan. Dōgen's community resided in the thatched-roof building of this abandoned temple while the nearby Daibutsu Monastery was under construction, 1243–1244.

Yuanwu Keqin: [Engo Kokugon]. 1063–1135, China. A dharma heir of Wuzu Fayan [Goso Hōen], Linji School. Also called Jiashan. Compiler of the *Blue Cliff Record.* Taught at Mt. Jia, Feng Region (Hunan). Given the titles of Zen Master Yuanwu and Zen Master Fuguo by the Emperors.

Yunju Daoying: [Ungo Dōyō] d. 902, China. A dharma heir of Dongshan Liangjie. Taught at Mt. Yunju, Hong Region (Jiangxi).

Yunmen School: A lineage from Yunmen Wenyan (864–949). One of the Five Schools of Zen in China.

Zen School: See "On the Endeavor of the Way" (p. xx) for Dōgen's view of its history.

Zhaozhou Congshen: [Jōshū Jūshin]. 778–897, China. A dharma heir of Nanquan Puyuan [Nansen Fugan], Qingyuan Line. Taught at the Guanyin Monastery, Zhao Region (Hebei). Posthumous name, Great Master Zhenji. Hero of numerous classic kōans.

Zhengjue: See *Hongzhi Zhengjue.*

Selected Bibliography

ENGLISH

Recommended Selections Specifically on Meditation

Anderson, Reb. *Being Upright: Zen Meditation and the Bodhi-sattva Precepts*. Berkeley: Rodmell Press, 2001.

Bielefeldt, Carl. *Dogen's Manuals of Zen Meditation*. Berkeley: University of California Press, 1988.

Cleary, Thomas, trans. and ed. *Minding Mind: A Course in Basic Meditation*. Boston: Shambhala, 1995.

Loori, John Daido, ed. *The Art of Just Sitting: Essential Writings on the Zen Practice of Shikantaza*. Boston: Wisdom Publications, 2002.

Nhat Hanh, Thich. *Miracle of Mindfulness: A Manual on Meditation*. Boston: Beacon Press, 1987.

Okumura, Shohaku, trans. and ed. *Shikantaza: An Introduction to Zazen*. Kyoto, Japan: Kyoto Soto Zen Center, 1985.

———, and Taigen Leighton, trans. *The Wholehearted Way: A Translation of Eihei Dogen's "Bendowa" with Commentary by Kosho Uchiyama Roshi*. Boston: Charles E. Tuttle and Company, 1997.

Books about Dogen

Abe, Masao. *A Study of Dogen: His Philosophy and Religion.*
Albany: State University of New York Press, 1992.

Bielefeldt, Carl. *Dogen's Manuals of Zen Meditation.* Berkeley:
University of California Press, 1988.

Cleary, Thomas, trans. *Rational Zen: The Mind of Dogen
Zenji.* Boston: Shambhala, 1993.

————, trans. *Record of Things Heard: The "Shobogenzo Zuimonki": Talks of Zen Master Dogen as Recorded by Zen
Master Ejo.* Boulder, Colo.: Prajna Press, 1980.

————, trans. *"Shobogenzo": Zen Essays by Dogen.* Honolulu:
University of Hawaii Press, 1986.

Cook, Francis. *How to Raise an Ox: Zen Practice as Taught in
Zen Master Dogen's "Shobogenzo."* Los Angeles: Center
Publications, 1978.

————. *Sounds of Valley Streams: Enlightenment in Dogen's
Zen.* Albany: State University of New York Press, 1989.

Eto, Sokuo. *Zen Master Dogen as Founding Patriarch.* Ichi-
mura, Shohei, trans. and ed., North American Institute
of Zen and Buddhist Studies, 2001.

Heine, Steven. *A Blade of Grass: Japanese Poetry and Aesthetics
in Dogen Zen.* New York: Peter Lang, 1989.

————. *Dogen and the Koan Tradition: A Tale of Two "Shobogenzo" Texts.* Albany: State University of New York Press,
1994.

————. *Existential and Ontological Dimensions of Time in
Heidegger and Dogen.* Albany: State University of New
York Press, 1985.

————. *The Zen Poetry of Dogen: Verses from the Mountain of
Eternal Peace.* Boston: Charles Tuttle and Co., 1997.

Jaffe, Paul, trans. *Flowers of Emptiness: Dogen's "Genjokoan"
with Commentary by Yasutani Roshi.* Boston: Shambhala,
1997.

Kim, Hee Jin. *Dogen Kigen: Mystical Realist.* Tucson: University of Arizona Press, 1975; Boston: Wisdom Publications, 2004.

———, trans. *Flowers of Emptiness: Selections from Dogen's "Shobogenzo."* Lewiston, N.Y.: Edwin Mellen Press, 1985.

Kodera, Takashi James. *Dogen's Formative Years in China: An Historical Study and Annotated Translation of the Hokyo-ki.* Boulder, Colo.: Prajna Press, 1980.

LaFleur, William R., ed. *Dogen Studies.* Honolulu: Kuroda Institute, University of Hawaii Press, 1985.

Leighton, Taigen Daniel, and Shohaku Okumura, trans. *Dogen's Pure Standards for the Zen Community: A Translation of Eihei Shingi.* Albany: State University of New York Press, 1996.

———, trans. *The Extensive Record of Eihei Dogen.* Boston: Wisdom Publications, 2004.

Masunaga, Reiho. *A Primer of Soto Zen: A Translation of Dogen's Shobogenzo Zuimonki.* Honolulu: University of Hawaii Press, 1978.

Merzel, Dennis Genpo. *Beyond Sanity and Madness: The Way of Zen Master Dogen.* Boston, Ruthland, Vermont, Tokyo: Charles Tuttle and Co., 1994.

Nishijima, Gudo Wafu, and Chodo Cross, trans. *Master Dogen's Shobogenzo.* 4 vols. Woods Hole, Mass.: Windbell Publications, 1994–1998.

Nishijima, Gudo, with Larry Zacchi and Michael Luetchford. *Master Dogen's Shinji Shobogenzo,* Book 1. Woods Hole, Mass.: Windbell Publications, 1990.

Nishiyama, Kosen, and John Stevens, trans. *Dogen Zenji's Shobogenzo (The Eye and Treasury of the True Law).* 4 vols. Sendai, Japan: Daihokkaikaku, 1975–1983.

Okumura, Shohaku, and Taigen Leighton, trans. *The Whole-hearted Way: A Translation of Eihei Dogen's "Bendowa" with Commentary by Kosho Uchiyama Roshi.* Boston: Charles Tuttle and Co., 1997.

Okumura, Shohaku, trans. and ed. *Dogen Zen*. Kyoto, Japan: Kyoto Soto Zen Center, 1988.

———, trans. *"Shobogenzo Zuimonki": Sayings of Eihei Dogen Zenji, Recorded by Koun Ejo*. Kyoto, Japan: Kyoto Soto Zen Center, 1987.

———, and Taigen Leighton, trans. *The Wholehearted Way: A Translation of Eihei Dogen's "Bendowa" with Commentary by Kosho Uchiyama Roshi*. Boston: Charles Tuttle and Co., 1997.

Shaner, David Edward. *The Bodymind Experience in Japanese Buddhism: A Phenomenological Study of Kukai and Dogen*. Albany: State University of New York Press, 1985.

Shimano, Eido, and Charles Vacher, trans. *Shobogenzo Bus-shô: the buddha nature/la nature donc bouddha*. La Versanne, France: Encre Marine, 2002.

———, trans. *Shobogenzo Uji: Être-temps, Being time*. La Versanne, France: Encre Marine, 1997.

———, trans. *Shobogenzo yui butsu yo butsu, shôji/seul boudha connaît bouddha, vie-mort*. La Versanne, France: Encre Marine, 1999.

Stambaugh, Joan. *Impermanence is Buddha-Nature: Dogen's Understanding of Temporality*. Honolulu: University of Hawaii Press, 1990.

Tanahashi, Kazuaki, ed. and trans. *Enlightenment Unfolds: The Essential Teachings of Zen Master Dogen*. Boston: Shambhala, 1999.

———, ed. and trans. *Moon in a Dewdrop: Writings of Zen Master Dogen*. New York: North Point Press, a division of Farrar, Straus and Giroux, 1985.

Waddell, Norman and Masao Abe, trans. with annotation. *The Heart of Dogen's Shobogenzo*. Albany: State University of New York Press, 2002.

Warner, Jisho, Shohaku Okumura, John McRae, and Taigen Dan Leighton, eds. *Nothing Is Hidden: Essays on Zen*

Master Dogen's Instructions for the Cook. New York: Weatherhill, 2001.

Wright, Thomas, trans. *Refining Your Life: From Zen Kitchen to Enlightenment, by Zen Master Dogen and Kosho Uchiyama*. New York: Weatherhill, 1983.

Yokoi, Yuho, trans. *The Shobogenzo*. Tokyo: Sankibo Buddhist Bookstore, 1986.

————, with Daizen Victoria. *Zen Master Dogen: An Introduction with Selected Writings*. New York: Weatherhill, 1976.

Books with Material Concerning Dogen

Aitken, Robert. *The Mind of Clover: Essays in Zen Buddhist Ethics*. New York: North Point Press, a division of Farrar, Straus and Giroux, 1984.

Anderson, Reb. *Being Upright: Zen Meditation and the Bodhisattva Precepts*. Berkeley: Rodmell Press, 2001.

————, *Warm Smiles from Cold Mountains: Dharma Talks on Zen Meditation*. Berkeley: Rodmell Press, 1999.

Bodiford, William M. *Soto Zen in Medieval Japan*. Honolulu: Kuroda Institute, University of Hawaii Press, 1993.

Cleary, Thomas, ed. and trans. *Timeless Spring: A Soto Zen Anthology*. Tokyo: Weatherhill, 1980.

————, trans. and ed. *Minding Mind: A Course in Basic Meditation*. Boston: Shambhala, 1995.

Cook, Francis, trans. *The Record of Transmitting the Light: Zen Master Keizan's Denkoroku*. Los Angeles: Center Publications, 1991.

Faure, Bernard. *Visions of Power: Imagining Medieval Japanese Buddhism*. Princeton, N.J.: Princeton University Press, 1996.

Habito, Ruben. *Healing Breath: Zen Spirituality for a Wounded Earth*. Dallas, Tex.: Maria Kannon Zen Center Publications, 1993.

Heine, Steven. *Shifting Shape, Shaping Text: Philosophy and*

Folklore in the Fox Koan. Honolulu: University of Hawaii Press, 1999.

———, and Dale Wright, eds., *The Koan: Texts and Contexts in Zen Buddhism.* Oxford, U.K.: Oxford University Press, 2000.

Kasulis, T. P. *Zen Action/Zen Person.* Honolulu: University of Hawaii Press, 1981.

Katagiri, Dainin. *Returning to Silence: Zen Practice in Daily Life.* Boston: Shambhala, 1988.

Leighton, Taigen Daniel. *Faces of Compassion: Classic Bodhisattva Archetypes and Their Modern Expressions.* Formerly published as *Bodhisattva Archetypes: Classic Buddhist Guides to Awakening and Their Modern Expressions.* New York: Penguin Arkana, 1998; revised edition, Boston: Wisdom Publications, 2003.

———, and Yi Wu, trans. *Cultivating the Empty Field: The Silent Illumination of Zen Master Hongzhi.* Originally published, Berkeley: North Point Press, 1991; revised, expanded edition, Boston: Charles Tuttle and Co., 2000.

Loori, John Daido, ed. *The Art of Just Sitting: Essential Writings on the Zen Practice of Shikantaza.* Boston: Wisdom Publications, 2002.

Nearman, Hubert, trans. *Buddhist Writings on Meditation and Daily Practice: The Serene Reflection Meditation Tradition.* Mount Shasta, Ca.: Shasta Abbey Press, 1994.

Okumura, Shohaku, trans. and ed. *Shikantaza: An Introduction to Zazen.* Kyoto, Japan: Kyoto Soto Zen Center, 1985.

———, and Thomas Wright, trans. *Opening the Hand of Thought.* New York: Viking Penguin, 1994.

Sato, Shunmyo. *Two Moons: Short Zen Stories.* Trans. by Rev. and Mrs. Shugen Komagata and Daniel Itto Bailey. Honolulu: The Hawaii Hochi, Ltd., 1981.

Sekida, Katsuki. *Zen Training: Methods and Philosophy.* New York: Weatherhill, 1996.

Snyder, Gary. *Mountains and Rivers without End*. Washington, D.C.: Counterpoint, 1996.

——, *The Practice of the Wild*. New York: North Point Press, a division of Farrar, Straus and Giroux, 1990.

Stone, Jacqueline. *Original Enlightenment and the Transformation of Medieval Japanese Buddhism*. Honolulu: University of Hawaii Press, 1999.

Suzuki, Shunryu, *Not Always So: Practicing the True Spirit of Zen*. New York: HarperCollins Publishers, 2002.

——, *Zen Mind, Beginner's Mind*. New York: Weatherhill, 1970.

Tanahashi, Kazuaki, and Tensho David Schneider, eds. *Essential Zen*. San Francisco: Harper, 1994.

Wenger, Michael, ed. *Windbell: Teachings from the San Francisco Zen Center 1968–2001*. Berkeley: North Atlantic Books, 2002.

Books in Japanese

Kawamura, Kodo, ed. *Eihei Kaisan Dogen Zenji Gyojo Kenzei-ki, Shohon Taiko (Kenzei's Biography of the Founder Dogen of Eihei, Comparative Version)*. Tokyo: Daishukan Shoten, 1975.

Masutani, Fumio, trans. *Gendaigo-yaku Shobogenzo (Modern Japanese Translation: Treasury of the True Dharma Eye).*, 8 vols. Tokyo: Kadokawa Shoten, 1973–1975.

Nakamura, Soichi, Sojun Nakamura, and Tanahashi, Kazuaki, trans. *Zen'yaku Shobogenzo (Complete Translation: Treasury of the True Dharma Eye)*, 4 vols. Tokyo: Seishin Shobo, 1971–1972.

Okubo, Doshu, ed. *Dogen Zenji Zenshu. (Entire Work of Zen Master Dogen)*, 3 vols. Tokyo: Chikuma Shobo, 1970.

Sakai, Tokugen, et al., ed. *Dogen Zenji Zenshu. (Entire Work of Zen Master Dogen)*, 7 vols. Tokyo: Shunjusha. 1988–1993.

Takeuchi, Michio. *Dogen*. Tokyo: Yoshikawa Kobunkan, 1962.